ON
FIFTH
AVENUE

THEN

AND

NOW

ON FIFTH AVENUE

THEN AND NOW

RONDA WIST

A BIRCH LANE PRESS BOOK
Published by Carol Publishing Group

A Birch Lane Press Book
Published by Carol Publishing Group
Birch Lane Press is a registered trademark of
Carol Communications, Inc.

Editorial Offices   Sales & Distribution Offices
600 Madison Avenue   120 Enterprise Avenue
New York, NY 10022   Secaucus, NJ 07094

In Canada: Canadian Manda Group
P.O. Box 920, Station U
Toronto, Ontario M8Z 5P9

Manufactured in the United States of America

10 9 8 7 6 5 4 3 2 1

Carol Publishing Group books are available at special discounts
for bulk purchases, for sales promotions, fund raising, or
educational purposes. Special editions can also be created to
specifications. For details contact: Special Sales Department,
Carol Publishing Group, 120 Enterprise Ave., Secaucus, NJ 07094

Design by Steven Brower

Cataloging Data for this publication can be obtained from the
Library of Congress

This book is dedicated with love to my remarkable mother—
REBA PSATY WIST

CONTENTS

CONTENTS
CONTINUED

CONTENTS
CONTINUED

ACKNOWLEDGMENTS

I think I have read—or at least glanced at—practically every *New York Times* article that mentions Fifth Avenue over the last eighty years. My immersion was complete when I began to mourn buildings and stores that died thirty years before my birth. Sometimes I felt as if I actually remembered Franklin Simon greeting his customers or the Red Cross nurses exercising on B. Altman's roof during World War I.

But every now and then reality would set in, when I would talk to people who truly remembered the avenue. I am so grateful to the countless shoppers who shared their stories and memories with me. They, better than the thousands of books and newspaper and magazine articles I read and reread, helped to explain what made the avenue so special. I would like to particularly thank the following wonderful people who took the time to talk to me, and in some cases lent personal photographs, some of which are published here for the first time: Eleanor Lambert Berkson, Seymour Durst, Sarah Tomerlin Lee, Leonard Hankin, Robert Hoskins, Elieth Roux, and Charles Scribner Jr. I also appreciate the assistance of Diana Feldman, Allan Johnson, Hilda Linden, and Josepha Miller.

The following people helped me to find, dig up, reprint and discover photographs: Brooke Adkins of FAO Schwarz, Diana Arecco and Pat Paladines of the New-York Historical Society, Anne Champagne of the Pattee Library at Pennsylvania State University, Helen Choi of the St. Regis Hotel, Tom Cusick and Raymond Small of the Fifth Avenue Association, Carla Fourie of Alfred Dunhill, Morgan Holman, the Verger at St. Thomas Church Fifth Avenue, Chuck Jones of the Plaza Hotel, Wendy Kassel of Cartier, Inc., Reva Kirschberg and Mark Heutlinger of Congregation Temple Emanu-El, Celine Lanza of Cushman and Wakefield, Alexandra Manolovici of Bergdorf Goodman, Dorothy Miner and Terri Rosen of the New York City Landmarks Preservation Commission, Helen O'Hagen, William Lorenzen and Julie Kurtzman of Saks Fifth Avenue, Eileen O'Meara of Bankers Trust, James Reed and Celeste Torello of the Rockefeller Group, Charles Scribner III, Joel Sherman of Nat Sherman, Christine Sloben of Tiffany & Co., Ellen Sowchek of the Pace University Archives, Elliott Taradash, Isabel Von Fluegge of Henri Bendel, Jan Walker and Bill Conard of Lord & Taylor, Barbara Washington of the Peninsula Hotel, and Daniel Weinreb and Bonnie Snow of Mall Properties.

I must thank the following people for doing all sorts of things, like undeleting lost chapters from the computer, giving me legal advice, and introducing me to people who knew about Fifth Avenue: Morris Sorkin, Robert Rice, Martin Psaty, Lee Seham, Michael Halle, Brenda Levin, Eustace Pilgrim, Edward Whitman, Michelle and Duane Desiderio, Lauren Otis, Jeanne Goodwin, Edan Heuckeroth, Sandy Hornick, Matthew Weinstein, Joan Klimo, Jeff Kemper, Candy Schulman, Michael Chin, Joy Bochner, James Dillon, John Young, Douglas Woodward, Amanda Burden, Lance Michaels, William Valetta. I'm particularly grateful to my brother Andrew Wist for his continued support.

My greatest thanks go to my researchers who spent months peering at microfilm and inserting thousands of coins into Xerox machines; my mother, Reba Psaty Wist, and her husband, Jerome Muchnick.

And, of course, I must thank my tranquilizers at Carol Publishing, the wonderful Allan J. Wilson and the fabulous Steven Brower.

Street of Dreams

Fifth Avenue was my yellow brick road lined with commercial palaces and dazzling display windows. Conservative B. Altman's at Thirty-fourth Street and opulent Bergdorf Goodman at Fifty-eighth Street were its sentinels. The breadth of the avenue and the great width of the store aisles gave me room to dream in the 1960s.

I could imagine being Judy Garland in *Easter Parade* or Audrey Hepburn in *Breakfast at Tiffany's*. My childhood fantasies ranged from wearing a black-and-white checked suit and pillbox hat like the young Peck and Peck Woman to a chartreuse minidress from Bergdorf's trendy Bigi department. These dreams are half-remembered, seen through the texture of a fabric rarely used, like silk organza.

On our shopping trips, my mother and I walked purposefully, amidst a swirl of stylish shoppers, visitors, and the occasional fashion model carrying a hatbox. We passed buildings that held the stores of my mother's young adulthood. She'd point and say, "That was Russeks, where I bought myself a sheared beaver coat because my mother told me that nice single girls didn't wear mink." She spoke of the postwar years, evoking names—Jay-Thorpe, Oppenheim Collins, The Tailored Woman—from a past I could barely imagine.

Open-topped double-decked buses snaked through two-way traffic, she told me. But the people on the upper deck—mostly romantic couples and tourists—never minded. She remembered the demolition of a Vanderbilt mansion on Fifty-first Street. "How could anyone live next door to Rockefeller Center?" I asked. Here and there a fragment of the residential past remained, like an overlooked artifact, surrounded by newer, taller buildings.

I had childish confidence that My Street would endure. With mahogany wainscoting, ornamented ceilings, and gleaming display cases, stores looked as if they had been standing for generations. The regal limestone spoke of permanence. Flags waving above the entrances welcomed foreign visitors. Men in suits hurried along

the avenue, but it belonged to women. The display windows enticed us, the perfume-scented vestibules invited us.

Only an earthquake, I thought, could destroy Bonwit Teller and DePinna, stores so posh that their charge account customers weren't burdened by carrying charge "plates." Best & Co.—whose barber sent home a lock of my hair from my first haircut—could never disappear. In Altman's, matrons in tweed suits looked as if they had been resting for centuries in the Ladies Lounge.

Surely, the high-heeled women wearing fitted fur coats in winter and dressmaker suits in spring would always glide into the stores. I imagined them buying cocktail dresses before lunching on the Upper East Side. Petulant boys in blue blazers holding mother's hand would *never* have a tantrum on the avenue. Casually dressed tourists, looking not quite like real New Yorkers, would stare at the buildings and ask the way to the Empire State Building or Saks Fifth Avenue. Young women would select silver patterns or gaze at the display windows filled with tulle and organdy puffs of bridal gowns.

New York's four seasons were reflected on the avenue. In December, the streets teemed with shoppers and tourists studying the Christmas windows, admiring Rockefeller Center's Christmas tree while buying chestnuts. In the winter evenings, the illuminated windows and Christmas decorations, the jostling crowds and the slushy roadway, made the avenue feel like a

small-town main street, or at least one in Brooklyn. The avenue was radiant in the spring: Sootless facades gleamed in the sunlight and people almost glowed as they walked beneath Lord & Taylor's colored awnings. The Easter Parade was a mile-long fashion show of gloved and hatted adults carefully eyeing other promenaders. In September, lead-footed women, pushed beyond endurance, grasped their children and their bags of back-to-school clothes. But during the summer, the avenue was almost serene. Contented visitors took over the avenue that glimmered in the heat.

I was certain that the avenue's rhythm would be fixed in time forever. On Sundays, the avenue was silent, resting, awaiting the new week. Parishioners gathered on the steps of the churches, and a few tourists strolled. Students taking a break from their wordy endeavors sat on the library steps. But the street looked sharp, clean, and empty, as in an Edward Hopper painting.

The avenue offered imperishable sanctuaries. Certainly, Schrafft's would always have tables of ancient translucent-skinned women sipping cocktails. Lord & Taylor's Birdcage would be filled with well-coifed women munching ladylike lunches at school desks.

After the 1960s ended, the avenue began to look like a dowager's forgotten necklace, with gems missing and settings broken. But now the necklace is being repaired. And we must treasure every jewel. Fifth Avenue is not a street that miraculously escapes damage. It has been fighting to hold onto its elegance for eighty years.

The closings of Best & Co., DePinna, and Bonwit Teller made Fifth Avenue less of a destination for many people. I was even sorry to see E. J. Korvette leave its majestic home. But the place that made me feel safe and secure was obviously permanent—B. Altman's. When that store closed, I recognized the end of my era—and with it, a thread that connected me to my mother and my mother's mother.

As an adult, I don't believe in the magic of Oz, but I believe that a day at Elizabeth Arden can do wonders. The grandeur of the avenue was not diminished because of my Lilliputian dreams—becoming Miss Bonwit or the Young Individualist was all I desired. Perhaps it was enhanced by such childhood thrills as my sitting next to Paulette Goddard in a posh beauty salon or standing behind an opera star on line at the passport office in Rockefeller Center.

Fifth Avenue rises up the crest of Murray Hill and beyond. At dusk, its ephemeral beauty is like an aging woman best seen by candlelight. The smoky glass facades dissolve, the limestone softens, the sky darkens, and the people withdraw. In sunlight, the flaws return, but the "good bones" of the avenue still hold it up—the glorious commercial palazzi, the library, the art deco skyscrapers, Rockefeller Center.

New York doesn't have many streets that inspire dreams. But Fifth Avenue can intoxicate us with fantasies—or memories.

There's always something tantalizing and just beyond reach—a string of pearls too expensive, a dress too tight, a pedestrian impossibly chic. And I hope this book helps some readers to vividly recall the avenue and others to dream anew.

I tried to imagine what it would be like to walk on Fifth Avenue with several generations of observant New Yorkers. What had the street been like? Who shopped where? Which buildings were here before?

It's time to take a stroll!

PART ONE

From Country Road to Millionaires' Mile

Overview

Less than a generation separated a brook-crossed road from an established thoroughfare lined with mansions. Many old New York families, like the Schermerhorns and Brevoorts, seemed content to remain in large, old-fashioned homes. On the other hand, many fashionable New Yorkers moved uptown to Union Square, Gramercy Park, or Madison Square. Meanwhile, the nouveaux riches moved farther north and tamed farms and suburbs into French chateaux and Renaissance palazzi. The avenue seemed to undergo an overnight metamorphosis, it didn't evolve—it sprang into full-blown existence.

After opening in the 1830s, Gramercy Park and Union Square immediately became fashionable. By midcentury, people built summer homes around Murray Hill, a spot high enough for cool breezes and distant views. Change came slowly to this northern outpost, but once development took hold, it was relentless. Farms were subdivided, roads were paved with cobblestones. By the end of the 1850s, the avenue had become a rural thoroughfare with grand suburban villas south of Forty-second Street.

However, there wasn't much of a market for the property between Forty-second and Fifty-ninth streets. Its terminus—Central Park—was an untamed, rutted mess until 1876. The avenue's inexpensive real estate and remoteness from fashionable downtown made it perfect for siting the grounds of public and private institutions and even cattle yards. So, it wasn't until the end of the century that homes were built near the park. After the construction hiatus during and after the Civil War, some wealthy residents moved northward away from the increasingly commercial Madison and Union squares.

By the last quarter of the nineteenth century, Fifth Avenue was a millionaires' village. Perhaps it was appropriate that families with new money found their homes on a new street, unsullied by a great deal of history. Some residents strengthened the roots of their family trees by marrying into old New York stock. But many of these people were self-made; rarely did more than a lifetime separate enormous wealth from its

creation. With the idea of the Four Hundred spawned in Mrs. Astor's home, gentlemen eating dinner on horseback in Sherry's, and Consuelo Vanderbilt marrying in St. Thomas Church, the avenue's residents created their own history.

Early Beginnings

Until the middle of the nineteenth century, Fifth Avenue was little more than a country road leading to Yorkville and beyond. Called the Middle Road, it was distinguished from the Albany Post Road to the west and the Boston (also called Eastern) Post Road.

The name Fifth Avenue appeared for the first time on the 1811 Commissioners Plan. The map charted downtown's ancient curved streets and superimposed a grid over Manhattan's erratic topographical features for the part of the city not yet developed. Still concentrated below Houston Street, New York City was little more than a congested provincial town. Greenwich Village was a fashionable suburb. The city took title to the properties that would become Fifth Avenue between Waverly Place and Thirteenth Street in 1824 and began building the street shortly thereafter. It wasn't until 1838 that the city took title to the properties that would become part of Fifth Avenue between Thirty-fourth and Fifty-ninth streets.

An 1840 map published by

London's Society for the Diffusion of Useful Knowledge delineated the city as far north as Forty-second Street. The "Downtown" was already developed with points of interest such as City Hall and Columbia College. Fifth Avenue was empty north of Madison Square, but for one small structure in the bed of the street. That house belonged to Lindley Murray, the son of the Murrays who lent their name to Murray Hill. During the Revolutionary War his mother had entertained and detained British officers, enabling generals Washington and Putnam to lead the pathetic Continental troops to safety in Harlem Heights.

Lindley's brother, John Murray, had purchased the land between Thirty-fifth and Thirty-seventh streets for $5,000 in 1804. It lay opposite the thirty-acre Bloomingdale farm; the surrounding area had changed little since his mother's act of heroism years before.

The Croton Distributing Reservoir

After disastrous fires destroyed much of downtown Manhattan, a number of protective measures were enacted, the most important of which was the creation of the Croton distributing reservoir at Forty-second Street. It was one of the city's greatest public works and put Fifth Avenue "on the map" for most New Yorkers. Until its construction, even the city's most elegant households got their water from the corner pump. That came to an end with the damming of Westchester's Croton River to create a reservoir. Traveling from Croton, the water flowed to the receiving reservoir at Eighty-sixth Street, and on to the distributing reservoir at Forty-second Street.

The immense, Egyptian-style enclosure surrounded a 20-million gallon "lake" opened in 1842. Its thick, battered walls (which receded as they rose) held a public promenade. Atop the fifty-foot-high walls, spectators could see Brooklyn, the Westchester hills, and the Palisades. Although some writers thought it "long continued to be one of the ugliest spots in the city," many disagreed. An 1866 guide to New York proclaimed it, "an imperishable monument to the glory of New York." When the reservoir opened, the celebratory banquet offered only one beverage—Croton water.

Fifth Avenue became the destination of strollers and coachmen out for afternoon drives. Stylish women wearing colorful bonnets would stroll at the fashionable time—between 12:00 A.M.. and 2:00 P.M.—from Madison Square to the reservoir and back. The avenue along the reservoir "served as a gentleman's race track"[1] on Saturday afternoons and Sunday mornings. This ephemeral monument was demolished less than sixty years later to make way for the New York Public Library.

In 1854, the Croton Cottage opened across the street from the reservoir. It dispensed refreshments, presumably stronger than those offered at the reservoir. It was adjacent to the Maze Garden, a labyrinth modeled on the one still in existence at England's Hampton Court.

During the Draft Riots of 1863, the city was under siege by an unruly crowd of rioters. They protested the unfair conscription which allowed wealthy men to buy their way out of the draft. For a few days, they tortured and killed blacks and whites. They ransacked Fifth Avenue. After attacking the Croton Cottage tavern, they moved on to the Colored Orphan Asylum. The four-story orphanage stood behind a garden on the west side of the avenue between Forty-fourth and Forty-fifth streets. Within minutes, the 1836 building was a ruin. Fortunately, it was empty; the 233 orphans had earlier been safely escorted to the police station house and then to the almshouse on Blackwell's Island. The asylum sold the property for $175,000 and moved to large, suburban grounds at One Hundred and Forty-third Street and Tenth Avenue.

Within a few years, the Croton Cottage site was purchased by William H. Vanderbilt for his first Fifth Avenue home. He later gave it to his son, Frederick W. Vanderbilt.

The draft rioters' meeting place was the Willow Tree Inn at the southeast corner of Forty-fourth Street. The son of the owner recollected years later that the building was spared—because his father ran the stage to downtown. This single means of public transportation was cheap and crude: When a passenger wanted a particular stop, he alerted the driver by pulling a strap attached to his legs.

By the end of the century, Fifth Avenue was traversed by horse-drawn omnibuses that traveled to Forty-second Street and Fifth Avenue from Fulton Ferry. An extra team of horses was brought to pull the vehicle up Murray Hill. The horse-drawn vehicles were replaced by electric buses at the turn of the century but they were not much faster.

Suburban Developments

As the western edge of fashionable Murray Hill, Fifth Avenue below Forty-second Street became a desirable suburb. Its farms and wide open spaces slowly disappeared beneath sporadic developments. Most of these first homes disappeared quickly, generally because the owners went bankrupt, or came close.

Amid farmlands and orchards, William Waddell built a turreted villa on the west side of the avenue at Thirty-seventh Street. President Andrew Jackson's friend surrounded his Gothic-style gray stucco house with vine-covered walls. Landscaped walks and gardens covered the entire blockfront.

The 1845 home remained only a few years, for in the Panic of 1857, Mr. Waddell sold the property to the Brick Presbyterian

Church. The church made a big move—from its home since 1767 on Park Row to a building designed by Leopold Eidlitz. This location was far north of its parishioners, but the streets of Murray Hill were starting to fill with the brownstones of the wealthy. The brick and brownstone church was appropriately simple; its interior was embellished at the end of the century by John LaFarge.

Fifth Avenue and Forty-second Street became a corner of exotic architectural styles. Facing the reservoir was architect Alexander Jackson Davis's House of Mansions, built in 1856. Extending from Forty-first to Forty-second streets, the Gothic-style facade with crenellated molding looked something like a castle. However, it contained eleven single-family residences. Despite its views and its interesting architecture, set behind deep front lawns, the project failed as a residential endeavor. In 1860, Rutgers Female College, the city's first seminary for the higher education of women, moved in. After the school moved to New Jersey, the row was slowly carved up between the 1880s and 1890s. One narrow slice remained in the middle until 1914, when it was absorbed into the site for the Rogers Peet & Co. building.[2]

In 1853, at the northwest corner of Thirty-fourth Street, a doctor built a house. Not just any doctor, this one had invented the drink "sarsaparilla" and so was known as Dr. "Sarsaparilla" Townsend. His spectacularly ugly home was a site included in guidebooks (after its completion, he

opened it to the public for a week). In a few years, it was sold and became a girls' school.

The brownstone pile was later sold to department store magnate A. T. Stewart in 1864. After demolishing it five years later, he built his pillared Marble Palace, designed by John Kellum. The mansard-roofed home with its rarely viewed art gallery and infrequently used ballroom was often criticized for its ostentation. Stewart died within a few years of its construction and his wife lived there until her death in 1886. In 1890, the Manhattan Club leased the building with much of its furniture and fittings.

Unlike the luxurious homes nearby, John Wendel's house, at the northwest corner of Thirty-ninth Steet, was built with a startlingly severe brick facade. The building was so stark that newspapers reported when new white lace curtains were hung at the windows. The 1856 house had a plain side yard behind a wall. Wendel, descended from John Jacob Astor I's partner in the fur business, lived there with his eccentric, unmarried sisters. Incredibly parsimonious, they were generous to their dogs, who had an enclosed dog run next to the house. Probably the least ornamented of all of the Fifth Avenue mansions, it had the longest life and lasted until the middle of the twentieth century.

Clubs and Trade

As residents moved north of Thirty-fourth

side streets.

And trade followed the affluent. It seemed that almost as soon as the avenue was lined with mansions, trade moved in—slowly, but at a steady pace. By 1885, Alfred DePinna opened a shop at 394 Fifth Avenue, next door to Mrs. Louis Hoyt's home on the northwest corner of Thirty-sixth Street (fig.5-1). DePinna had begun importing English sailor suits for his sons and later began selling copies. In 1889, J.N.A. Griswold sold his brownstone at 355 Fifth Avenue (on the northeast corner of Thirty-fourth Street) to the Knoedler Gallery. This was a fashionable spot for an important gallery—within a block or two of the stylish decorating firm, Herter Brothers, and the art

Fig. 5-1 View north, along west side of Fifth Avenue from Thirty-sixth Street. Mrs. Louis Hoyt's brownstone at the corner is adjacent to a converted residence painted white that is occupied by Alfred DePinna's shop. Next door to the boys' outfitter is the Singer Sewing Machine store. The Brick Presbyterian Church stands at the Thirty-seventh Street corner with Franklin Simon's original shop adjacent to it.
Courtesy: Private Collection

Street, churches, clubs, and hotels followed, leaving the downtown areas bereft of social standing. The avenue below Forty-second Street was crowded with the mansions of Austin Corbin, president of the Long Island Rail Road and founder of Manhattan Beach, Governor E. D. Morgan, various Kips, and P. T. Barnum. An 1879 map depicts the avenue below Forty-second Street starting to fill up with houses that often had stables alongside them, before prohibitive prices and restrictive covenants forced the stables to

Fig. 5-2 View north, along east side of the avenue from Thirty-ninth Street. The Union League Club, designed in the Queen Anne style, dominates the northeast corner of Thirty-ninth Street. Courtesy: Private Collection

gallery of Durand-Ruel.

Clubs also followed the affluent, and left their premises near Union and Madison squares. By the end of the century, many recently vacated mansions had become exclusive clubhouses. The City Club, organized as an "anti-bad-city government" club, was at Thirty-fifth Street. The St. Nicholas Club, at Thirty-sixth Street, required that proposed members be descendants of a resident of the city or state prior to 1785. The New-York Club moved into the ivy-covered Caswell mansion at Thirty-fifth Street. The Lotos Club, with membership limited to five hundred, half of whom were to be members of the "musical and dramatic professions," moved to a large brownstone at Forty-fifth Street. The Delta Kappa Epsilon Society had a home at Thirty-ninth Street. The Republican Club was at Fortieth Street, and the Democratic Club had a townhouse at Fiftieth Street. The New Club occupied 747 and 749 Fifth Avenue. For a while in the 1870s, the Metropolitan Museum moved to a temporary home at 681 Fifth Avenue, formerly Dodsworth's Dancing Academy.

The Union League Club constructed its house in the Queen Anne style, designed by Peabody & Stearns, in 1881 (fig.5-2). At the northeast corner of Thirty-ninth Street, it was considered the finest clubhouse at the time, with interiors decorated by John LaFarge and Tiffany Studios. It was famous for its club library and monthly receptions, showing American and European paintings, which were open to guests. Organized during the Civil War in support of the president of the United States, the club required all members to be loyal to the federal government. With the end of the Civil War, the Union League became the embodiment of the Republican Party aims and the newly created Manhattan Club reflected Democratic goals.

Early Developments North of Forty-second Street

Without the residential influence from Murray Hill, the area north of Forty-second Street took longer to be developed. Even through the 1860s and 1870s, when the city was growing steadily northward, the avenue retained a somewhat bucolic quality. Ponds, located at intervals along the avenue, were operated by private skating clubs. In those winters, much colder and longer than ours, spectators would drive out on sleighs to watch the skaters skim along the sites of the future Plaza Hotel and W. & J. Sloane. Although institutional uses predominated, mansions began to appear in force after the Civil War. And Forty-second Street always had a commercial flavor: The Forty-second Street crosstown surface cars traveled from ferry to train depot—river to river.

In 1801, Dr. David Hosack, a Columbia College professor, bought a large property from the city. Three years later, on twenty acres bounded by Forty-seventh and Fifty-first streets, and Fifth and Sixth avenues, he opened the Elgin Botanical Gardens. The site contained two thousand plant species, a large greenhouse, and two hothouses.

New York State later purchased the site and in 1814, as an aid-to-education act, deeded it to Columbia College (later University). Moving uptown to Forty-ninth Street and Madison Avenue, the University leased this "upper estate" for residential development. The new brownstones were

Fig. 7-1 Temple Emanu-El, at the northeast corner of Forty-third Street, drawn when it was the area's tallest and most commanding building. Courtesy: Congregation Emanu-El of the City of New York

elegant and soon occupied by notable New Yorkers; one of the side streets became known as Doctors' Row.

When a brownstone mansion was built on the northeast corner of Fifty-second Street in the 1850s, the area was a veritable wilderness. The occupant was Madame Restell, possibly the city's most famous abortionist. Despite innuendo and scandal, she remained, shunned by society, but presumably necessary to it. Finally, in 1878, she was arrested as a result of the efforts of Anthony Comstock and the Society for the Suppression of Vice. By then, the avenue was filled with the homes of the city's wealthiest citizens. She committed suicide before going to trial.

Houses of Worship

By 1879, there were eight houses of worship between Thirty-fifth and Fifty-fifth streets, most of which moved from increasingly crowded and deteriorated downtown neighborhoods. Of these fashionable and wealthy congregations, some were over one hundred years old, whereas a couple found

their very first home on the avenue.

Old pictures suggest that the northeast corner of Forty-third Street was fairly rural. It was the site that one of the city's most affluent German Jewish congregations selected for its house of worship in 1868 (fig.7-1). The Temple Emanu-El congregation had been organized in 1845 and had met in a remodeled courtroom and later a church on the Lower East Side. A nineteenth-century guidebook noted that "like all the finer Jewish synagogues of the city, it is Moorish in design and decoration."[3] Architect Leopold Eidlitz designed an exotic, Saracenic style yellow-and-brown sandstone building with red and black tiles on the roof. Its sanctuary held seats for two thousand. Samuel Adler, father of Yiddish theater actor Felix Adler, served as rabbi for many years. By the end of the nineteenth century, it was the only reform synagogue that held Sunday as well as Saturday services.

The Church of the Heavenly Rest, little wider than the abutting mansions, inspired one wag to say, "I see the heavenly . . . where's the rest?" (fig.7-2). The church, located at 551 Fifth Avenue, had figures of angels blowing trumpets standing on its cornice. Its services were originally held in the Rutgers Female College in 1865. The interior of the fashionable church was richly designed with frescoed walls and stained glass windows.

Columbia sold the corner of Forty-eighth Street to the Fifth Avenue Collegiate Church of St. Nicholas, which was dedicated

in 1872. The bell in its tower had originally hung in the Middle Dutch Church on Nassau Street. Of Newark sandstone, the Gothic-style building had a tall spire on the Forty-eighth Street corner balanced by flying buttresses and a small spire to the north.

Delmonico's and Sherry's

In the beginning of the nineteenth century, Isaac Burr owned the property on the east side of the avenue between Forty-second and Forty-fourth Streets. The northeast corner of Forty-second Street was later occupied by the Hamilton Hotel and later, Levi P. Morton's home. Converted to commercial use, it was recently demolished.

Near the corner of Forty-third Street, 511 Fifth Avenue had been the brownstone home of "Boss" Tweed before his family moved to Madison Avenue. It later became the home of Robert T. Wilson, a Southerner who had become wealthy by selling blankets to the Confederate army. The parvenu's charming children married affluent spouses, including a Vanderbilt and an Astor, and several lived on Fifth Avenue.

A cattle yard stood between Forty-fourth and Forty-sixth Streets until 1840, with the northeast corner of Forty-fourth Street occupied by a low frame hotel. After the business had moved to the West Side, the hotel property was eventually purchased by John H. Sherwood for a family hotel called

Sherwood House. A real estate developer, Sherwood also founded the Fifth Avenue Bank. The bank was the first to welcome women—ones who could keep account balances of at least $25,000. In 1875, he allowed the bank, one of the avenue's earliest, to rent his basement as its first home. In 1890, Sherwood sold the property for $635,000 (a bit less than $70 per square foot) to Theodore A. Havemeyer.

He, with Charles Delmonico, built the uptown Delmonico's. Opened in 1897, the limestone, brick, and terra cotta building was designed in the Italian Renaissance style by James Brown Lord. With a small garden on Fifth Avenue, the main entrance was on Forty-fourth Street. The light blue Ladies' Restaurant and Palm Garden were on the ground floor. The dining rooms were on the second floor and the rose-tinted ballroom was on the third floor. Two floors of bachelor apartments extended along the Fifth Avenue frontage on the upper floors. Within two years, a tear-filled farewell dinner was held at the Delmonico's at Madison Square. Its closing was a sure sign that society had moved uptown.

A year after the uptown Delmonico's opened, his competitor for the carriage trade, Louis Sherry, moved uptown and opened his establishment on the opposite corner. Designed by McKim, Mead & White, the twelve-story building contained beautifully decorated

public rooms, large bachelor apartments, and a landscaped outdoor café on the avenue. The conspicuous consumers of the "Gay Nineties" found the perfect place for their extravaganzas, like the famous and odoriferous Dinner on Horseback where guests rode their mounts into the dining room, drank champagne, and ate a banquet while servants ran around cleaning up the droppings. Mrs. Astor gave a ball to baptize the restaurant into society. The constant schedule of parties, balls, and teas brought Mr. Sherry so much success that he was able to purchase a home on Long Island which one of the Vanderbilts later purchased from him.

Fig. 9-1 View of east side of the avenue looking north from Forty-sixth Street, ca. 1905. Despite the proximity of the commercial Windsor Arcade, this portion of the avenue remained solidly residential, with high stoops, are aways, and street trees. The Gould home, with cresting on the mansard roof, is nearest the camera; the Goelet house is at the far corner of the block. The spires of St. Patrick's Cathedral are visible in the background. Courtesy: Private Collection

Life on the Avenue

In the 1870s and 1880s Fifth Avenue became home to many wealthy businessmen. They lived in solid Victorian comfort in brownstone mansions. In 1880, brothers Robert and Ogden Goelet commissioned architect Edward Hale Kendall to design residences at 589 and 608 Fifth Avenue, respectively. The Goelet family owned large parcels on the avenue, in part because two daughters of an avenue landowner had married into the family in the early nineteenth century.

One of the avenue's less ostentatious homes, 579 Fifth Avenue, belonged to Jay Gould, the wealthy financier (fig.9-1). His shady past—part rumor, mostly true—was that he had made his fortune by using inside information, making illicit deals, and as a result had ruined many innocent investors.

He was a very clever man who won the battle for the Erie Railroad despite Commodore Vanderbilt's attempts to stop him. But he is perhaps best remembered for his role in 1869's Black Friday. Gould manipulated the price of gold by purchasing millions of dollars worth of the precious metal. Then he persuaded President Grant's brother-in-law to help him, by ensuring that the government would not stop his attempt at cornering the gold market. When the president discovered what his brother-in-law had done, he was slow to act. So for two days, Gould sold his gold at inflated prices, while appearing to buy. Investors followed his apparent path. The price of gold continued to rise and Gould was getting richer as he was selling it. On Friday, President Grant released five million dollars worth of gold for sale and the prices plummeted. The Stock Exchange closed for a short time, to "separate the solvent from the ruined."[4]

Despised and reviled, Gould went on to other ventures. With his Fifth Avenue neighbor Russell Sage, he took over the country's most valuable telegraph system. He built Lyndhurst, his Gothic estate overlooking the Hudson River in Irvington, New York, and also a yacht, for a quarter of a million dollars. When he died of consumption in 1892, he left more than $75 million to his family.

Helen, the oldest daughter, remained in the house after the deaths of her parents and looked after her three younger siblings. She appeared to spend the remainder of her life repenting for her father's deeds by giving vast amounts of money to charity and educational institutions.

In the 1860s, two "rows" of houses were built on the east side of the street: Marble Row and the Colford-Jones Block. In 1823, John Mason, one of the founders of Chemical Bank, purchased eight large parcels of property, between Fifty-fourth and Sixty-third streets and Fifth and Fourth (now Park) avenues. He paid approximately $10 a lot, with parcels 200 feet by 950 feet sold for $2,500. When he died several years later, his will revealed that he had cut off his son, Henry Mason, with an annuity of $2,500 for the sin of marrying an actress. The contested will was in the courts for fifteen years. The distribution of wealth resulted in two remarkable works of architecture. His eldest daughter, Mrs. Mary Mason Jones, received the block between Fifty-seventh and Fifty-eighth streets and another relative, Mrs. Colford Jones, was given the block between Fifty-fifth and Fifty-sixth Streets.

Mary Mason Jones, an aunt of Edith Wharton (née Jones) hired Robert Mook to design Marble Row in 1867 (fig.9-2). The white marble-fronted homes with mansard roofs looked very Parisian. Although the area was considered too uptown to be fashionable, Mrs. Jones moved into the corner house at Fifty-seventh Street. The project was a success and was always occupied by prominent New Yorkers. By the end of the century, the Seventh Regiment Veteran Club had moved into the northern house at Fifty-eighth Street.

In 1869, Detlef Lienau designed eight large houses built behind the unified brownstone facade of the Colford-Jones block between Fifty-fifth and Fifty-sixth

Fig. 9-2 View of east side of the avenue looking north from Fifty-seventh Street. Edith Wharton's aunt, Mrs. Mary Mason Jones, commissioned this marble row of houses, and lived in the Fifty-seventh Street corner house. She slept in a bedroom on the ground floor because she was too obese to walk up and down the stairs. The original Hotel Savoy may be seen in the distance. Courtesy: Private Collection

streets. Mrs. Colford Jones occupied the house at the northeast corner of Fifty-fifth Street, which adjoined the house of her daughter-in-law Mrs. Lewis Jones. The main rooms of their houses could be joined together for large social functions. A daughter, Helen and her husband Woodbury Langdon, a grandson of John Jacob Astor, lived in the house at the corner of Fifty-sixth Street. Eventually the entire block came into the Langdon family.

The Windsor Hotel

The Windsor Hotel was built in 1873 on the east side of the avenue between Forty-sixth and Forty-seventh Streets (fig.10-1). Predating the Waldorf-Astoria and more modern than the Fifth Avenue Hotel on Twenty-third Street, it was the aristocratic uptown hotel. The grand hotel, unlike the small family hostelries on the avenue, became a fashionable meeting place in part because of its proximity to the homes of many financiers. Jay Gould lived across the street and therefore frequently visited this "uptown center of commerce," perhaps a bit more often than Russell Sage, Henry Flagler, and W. H. Vanderbilt. Before he was married, Andrew Carnegie lived there; it was President McKinley's New York hotel—where a special telephone was hooked up with Washington for him.

Despite the hotel's beauty, it was not fireproofed. On Saint Patrick's Day in 1899, a hotel guest stood in a front parlor watching the parade. After lighting a cigarette (or cigar), he tossed the blazing match to the street. At that moment the lace curtains blew into the room. They caught fire and the guest turned and ran. Passing by, the hotel's headwaiter saw the incident and tried to extinguish the blaze. His abortive attempt ended with his hands burned and the fire spreading to the walls. After wasting time in the hotel office, he ran into the street.

His yells of "Fire!" were drowned out by the sounds of the parade. As smoke poured out of the windows, the crowd finally noticed (fig.10-2).

The fire rapidly progressed through wide halls, vestibules, and elevator shafts. Chaos reigned as people tried desperately to escape. Some slid down ropes hung from their bedrooms, but the friction against their hands caused them to lose their grip. Guests and workers jumped off windowsills to their death on the street. Some guests escaped down two fire escapes along the rear wall. Others jumped from the roof to an adjoining roof on Forty-seventh Street. The Fire Department had difficulty getting through the parade-blocked avenue, but once there, acted swiftly and with heroism. However, the water supply was poor and their result thereby limited. An hour after the flames were discovered, the building was gutted.

The cornice of Miss Helen Gould's house was scorched. She generously had cots set up in her house for the injured; some of the seriously wounded workers and guests died in her front parlor.

For days, thousands of New Yorkers came to view the ghoulish cleanup of the ruins. No live bodies were discovered, but for a small whimpering dog that may have actually escaped *into* the rubble after the fire. The Lotos Club, across the street at 556 Fifth Avenue, reported that one thousand people applied for membership to have better viewing of the operations. After it was determined that no bodies remained, the hulk was dynamited.

Although the building was a firetrap, without a single fireproof stairway, it complied with appropriate codes. As usual, after the tragedy, building codes were amended and made more stringent.

Upper Fifth Avenue

Upper Fifth Avenue waited until after the Civil War for any significant development. Below Fifty-first Street stood the New York Institute for the Instruction of the Deaf and Dumb. On the southeast corner of Fiftieth Street, the Buckingham Hotel, a quiet family place, was built in 1877. The Democratic Club moved to a town house next door.

Above Fifty-first Street was the Roman Catholic Orphan Asylum. For $1.00 a year, it had been granted 450 feet between Fifty-first and Fifty-second streets. The four-story brick "boys building" accommodated 500 boys. Completed in 1851, it stood behind beautifully landscaped grounds.

Between Fifty-fourth and Fifty-fifth streets was St. Luke's Hospital, which remained from 1858 until its 1895 move to the Upper West Side. The sick poor were treated at this "most homelike" of the local hospitals. It had been an idea of the Episcopal rector of the Church of the Holy Communion. When the hospital opened, the Reverend Dr. William Muhlenberg actually moved into the building.

In the midst of all this, the cornerstone of St. Patrick's Cathedral was laid in 1858, in front of seven bishops and approximately one hundred thousand onlookers (fig. 11-1) Construction was halted during the Civil War and the church was not formally opened until 1879, although the towers were still incomplete. When construction began, the area was vacant; by the time the church opened, it was in the midst of the city's most fashionable district.

James Renwick Jr. designed the outstanding marble Gothic Revival church above a base of granite. With the cardinal's residence and rectory on Madison Avenue, and the Lady Chapel added in 1906, the cathedral occupied the entire city block. With 330-foot-high spires, a 26-foot-diameter rose window, profuse decoration of stained glass, and delicate tracery, the building must have been an awesome inspiration to the thousands of recent immigrants who had flooded into the city.

Other churches followed: In 1875, the Fifth Avenue Presbyterian Church moved from Nineteenth Street to Fifty-fifth Street. The "plain but handsome" brownstone church became known as the "Church of the Millionaires," not only for its wealthy parishioners, but also because its pastor was rumored to make a salary of $40,000 and charge $1,000 for weddings

Fig. 10-2 View of the Windsor Hotel fire taken on St. Patrick's Day, March 17, 1899. Smoke billows from upper floors and water from the fire hose barely reaches the second floor. The structure was not required to be fireproofed, but building codes were modified after this tragedy. Photograph: Fred H. Smyth. Courtesy: The New-York Historical Society

Fig. 10-1 View of east side of the avenue looking north from Forty-fifth Street, ca. 1890s. The Windsor Hotel with its outdoor café, known as a "summer garden," is shown on a summer day. Jay Gould, who lived in the house across Forty-seventh Street, frequented the hotel, known as the "uptown center of commerce." Courtesy: Private Collection

Fig. 11-1 View south from Fifty-second Street shows east side of the avenue, ca. 1890s. St. Patrick's Cathedral towers between the beautifully landscaped Roman Catholic Orphan Asylum to the north and the Buckingham Hotel to the south. Courtesy: Private Collection

and funerals.[5]

In 1870, St. Thomas Church moved from Broadway and Houston Street to the northwest corner of Fifty-third Street and Fifth Avenue (fig.11-2). The congregation, which had been founded in 1823, moved into a brownstone Gothic church designed by Richard Upjohn, one of the city's foremost ecclesiastical architects. The interior was crowded with masterworks, such as paintings by LaFarge and reredos by St. Gaudens that ornamented an apsidal chancel, and extravagant stained glass

windows. The chime of the bells in the tower "rivaled those of Trinity in sweetness."[6] The church was particularly known for its assistance to the city's poor.

Although the surrounding area was sparsely developed at the time, the church was soon in the middle of the Vanderbilt Colony, and, as always, played a great part in high society events (fig.11-3). Consuelo Vanderbilt married the duke of Marlborough in 1895 and President Benjamin Harrison married Mary Scott Dimmick in 1896 in the church.

The current verger, Morgan Holman, explains that the Easter Parade had its beginnings at St. Thomas Church. After the 11:00 A.M. Easter Sunday service, parishioners would carry the altar flowers to the patients at the nearby St. Luke's Hospital. The streets became crowded with the servants of the rich—eager to see what

everyone else's mistress was wearing. Until modern times, this fashion show was a major media event abundantly covered in the Monday newspapers and the following Sunday's rotogravure sections.

The Vanderbilt Colony

By the 1880s and 1890s, a few blocks of Fifth Avenue became known as the "Vanderbilt Colony" (fig.12-1). It seems strange to modern eyes that the Vanderbilt family would build their homes in the midst of institutions, but fashion was pushing ever northward, and people like Andrew Carnegie built even farther up in the hinterlands, on East Nintieth Street, amid vast areas of vacant land. As the United States government was attempting to colonize the world, the Vanderbilts colonized Fifth Avenue.

An observer noted that the very rich lived "with a complication of domestic machinery about them approximating that of the royal families of Europe

Fig. 11-2 View north from East Fifty-second Street, ca. 1880. The area around the recently constructed St. Thomas Church is quite undeveloped; the Vanderbilt homes have not yet been built. The trees stand in front of St. Lukes Hospital; the Fifth Avenue Presbyterian Church is in the distance. The imposing mansion in the foreground had belonged to Madame Restell, an abortionist. Courtesy: Archives of St. Thomas Church-Fifth Avenue

and closely resembling that of the great noble houses of England."[7] These gigantic mansions, designed in increasingly regal styles, were showcases for wealth with ever grander ballrooms, more detailed ceilings, more ornate carvings, rarer marbles, more crowded art galleries, and larger state dining rooms. Yet these museums were inhabited generally little more than a few weeks a year.

After the death of Commodore Cornelius Vanderbilt, his eldest son William H. and his wife Louise Kissam moved up the avenue in 1882. The northwest corner of Fifty-first Street had been most recently occupied by a farmhouse set behind a vegetable garden that provided produce to the families on lower Fifth Avenue. The Roman Catholic Orphan Asylum was across the avenue.

Architect John B. Snook designed two buildings as a unit for three families. The elder Vanderbilts' mansion at 640 Fifth Avenue shared an entrance vestibule with the one adjoining occupied by their daughter Emily and her husband William Sloane. Daughter Margaret and her husband Colonel Elliott F. Shepard entered their home at Two West Fifty-second Street. The massive, four-story, seventy-five-foot-high mansions of brownstone quarried from Connecticut were rumored to cost more than $2 million. Supposedly, six hundred construction workers worked day and night on the buildings, known by most as the "Twin Houses" and snidely called by some the "Twin Horrors."

The buildings were grim and

Fig. 11-3 View of St. Thomas Church, ca. 1900. By this time, the Vanderbilt Colony surrounds St. Thomas Church. A block north of the church the new University Club has been built on a portion of the St. Lukes property. The Fifth Avenue Presbyterian Church stands at Fifty-fifth Street. Courtesy: Archives of St. Thomas Church-Fifth Avenue

overbearing despite elaborately ornamented bronze doors modeled on Ghiberti's fifteenth century doors to the Baptistery facing the Duomo in Florence and stained glass windows by John LaFarge. Much of the fifty-eight-room interior was designed by Charles B. Atwood of the Herter Brothers decorating firm. The art gallery, cluttered with paintings and the subject of the privately printed *Mr. Vanderbilt's House and Collection*, was open to the public one day a week. Leaving nothing to chance, for the sidewalk Vanderbilt imported huge twelve-inch-thick slabs of blue slate from Vermont which weighed up to thirty tons each. (They

were destroyed with difficulty in 1957 by the Tishman Company when it was preparing the site for an office building.)

Continuing to sow the seeds of his colony, Vanderbilt had two more houses designed by Snook for his daughters: a Gothic mansion for Lila and William Seward Webb at 680 Fifth Avenue, adjacent to St. Thomas, and a Renaissance design for Florence and Hamilton Twombly at 684 Fifth Avenue. When William H. Vanderbilt died in 1885, his youngest son George received 640 Fifth Avenue. He continued to live there with his mother; by the time she died in 1896, he was spending most of his time at

Biltmore, his estate in North Carolina.

William Henry's second son, William Kissam Vanderbilt and his wife, the former Alva Smith of Mobile, hired Richard Morris Hunt to design the city's first Francois I chateau at West Fifty-second Street, across the street from George. Notable among its lavish appointments were a Persian-Moorish smoking room, carved wood ceilings, and a bathtub hewn from a solid block of flawless marble valued at $50,000. Ultimately, several works of art, including a secretary that had belonged to Marie Antoinette, tapestries, and a painting by Rembrandt, were bequeathed to the Metropolitan Museum of Art.

The $3 million turreted limestone building was the site of Mrs. Vanderbilt's ball for twelve hundred socialites. Alva excluded Mrs. William Astor with the excuse that they had never been introduced. Mrs. Astor acquiesced to her daughter Carrie's desire to attend the party and left her card at Mrs. Vanderbilt's home. The Astors were invited and the Vanderbilts had scored a social coup.

The willful Mrs. Vanderbilt forced her beautiful but malleable daughter Consuelo into a miserable marriage with the impoverished but titled ninth duke of Marlborough. Despite her social successes, Alva soon left the chateau when she divorced Vanderbilt to marry Oliver Hazard Perry Belmont, a man several years younger. After Belmont's death, she took up many causes, including that of women's suffrage, and led many parades up Fifth Avenue

Fig.12-1 View north from East Fifty-first Street shows west side of the avenue. This shows much of the Vanderbilt Colony: At the left is the northern "Twin House" and across Fifty-second Street is William K. Vanderbilt's chateau. The towers of St. Thomas Church and the Fifth Avenue Presbyterian Church are visible. The fence on the right is in front of the Roman Catholic Orphan Asylum. Courtesy: Private Collection

espousing that cause. At her funeral service at St. Thomas Church, her coffin was borne by female pallbearers (as she had requested). William K. enjoyed the rest of his life as a peripatetic sportsman and died in 1920 in France at the Auteuil Race Track at the age of seventy.

William K. Vanderbilt Jr. and his wife, Virginia Graham Fair, moved into a chateau next door. Stanford White's design for 666 Fifth Avenue was rather stately and not overblown.

Even more magnificent than these chateaux, however, was the chateau (based on either the Chateau de Blois or the Chateau de Chenonceau) built by William K.'s older brother Cornelius Vanderbilt II and his wife, Alice Gwynne[8] (fig.12-2). While living on Fifth Avenue and Thirty-second Street in the 1870s, Vanderbilt began assembling his uptown property. In 1878, he purchased a corner brownstone, with its stable at One West Fifty-seventh Street, for approximately $100,000. He continued to add other Fifth Avenue houses and built his home on the Fifty-seventh Street corner. When his father died in 1885, Cornelius became the de facto head of the family. Soon thereafter he began to enlarge his house. In 1887, after deciding to build a grander residence, he purchased the Fifty-eighth Street frontage of the block for approximately $900,000.

His house was begun in 1882 and completed in 1893. The architectural firm of George B. Post and Sons created models of the building at the French Chateau de Blois,

by special permission of the French government. The splendid interior was not faithful to a particular period, but was planned for lavish entertaining. The immense ballroom was decorated in the Louis XIV style; the salon in the Louis XV style, and another room was designed in the Moorish style after Mr. Post spent a month in Granada, Spain. As Americans were plundering Europe for its works of art, the Vanderbilts were importing pieces of buildings as well. When the parquet floors, moldings, and other trim were brought to this country from France, the seams opened because of the temperature change. Chandelier and lighting fixtures were copied from French chateaux and the patterns were destroyed after use. The outdoor space between the caryatid-supported porte cochere and the fences was occupied by a large lawn, a driveway, and formal gardens (inadvertently affording passersby what we would now call a "visual amenity").

Across Fifty-seventh Street was the "much more modest, but still palatial" home of Vanderbilt's son-in-law, H. Payne Whitney. Railroad magnate Collis Huntington's gray palace was across the avenue, guarded by pillars topped by stone lions.

The Vanderbilts were able to keep odious uses and people at bay. But even as they were spending fortunes beautifying their homes, trade was edging little by little up the avenue. Not encroaching upon them, of course, but coming ever closer. In the 1890s, a number of genteel hotels were

constructed near the southern entrance of Central Park. The Plaza was built in 1890 and was quickly followed by the Savoy and the Netherland (fig.12-3). With their proximity to Central Park, mansions and fine clubs, these hotels quickly attracted a high-society crowd and established the area as a hotel hub.

As the Vanderbilt Chateau was nearing completion, William Waldorf Astor had left his home over a mile away. As a way of finally getting back at his aunt who insisted on calling herself The Mrs. Astor, despite the presence of his wife, he had a hotel constructed on the site of his mansion. And Fifth Avenue took a giant step toward the future.

The hotel, named after the town of Waldorf, the Astor family's ancestral home, opened on Thirty-third Street in 1893 (fig.12-4). Its shadows and noise made living next door intolerable for Mrs. William B. Astor. She and her son, John Jacob Astor IV, moved to Sixty-fifth Street and in 1897 erected the Astoria, on Thirty-fourth Street, named after a town in Oregon founded by an

Opposite
Fig.12-2 View south, from East Fifty-eighth Street, of the Cornelius Vanderbilt chateau with its West Fifty-eighth Street porte cochere, ca. 1920s. This is just one of Fifth Avenue's many mansions that were demolished after one generation of use. This photograph was taken shortly before the fifty-eight-room chateau was torn down. Vanderbilt's widow, Alice Gwynne Vanderbilt, complained of being hemmed in by trade, such as the twenty-five-story Heckscher Building across Fifty-seventh Street. Contrast this photograph with previous views of the formerly tranquil Vanderbilt Colony. Bergdorf Goodman is now on this site. Courtesy: Bergdorf Goodman

Astor. More magnificent than its predecessor, it was connected to it, thereby benefiting both sets of Astors. It was the largest, most glamorous hotel yet constructed in a city that was getting used to ostentation. It caused a stir: it was huge, its appointments were opulent, and unescorted women were allowed to be guests.

The spectacular ballrooms and private rooms became the city's premier gathering places. The sixteen-story hotel had thirteen hundred bedrooms and seven hundred baths. It had three grand ballrooms, and smaller rooms like the Astor Gallery, a concert and dance hall, and the Turkish Room, a dark exotic space where coffee was served by a "genuine" Turk. The hotel was a massive hive of activity. It was a spectacle with staff and visitors whirling around. Visitors gave their cards to desk clerks, who had them conveyed by pneumatic tube to the proper floor, where they were was taken by a boy to the appropriate chambers.

The public rooms were—alarmingly—democratic and public. Peacock Alley was a long, narrow corridor lined with benches where anyone could sit for hours to watch and be seen. A three-story atriumlike space was called the Garden Court of Palms. In summer, there was a special roof garden; in winter, part of it was flooded for rooftop ice-skating.

Opposite
Fig. 12-3 Winter view from West Fifty-eighth Street shows the Netherland Hotel at Fifth Avenue and East Fifty-ninth Street. Courtesy: Private Collection

The Bradley Martins, a wealthy couple from upstate New York, threw a party in 1897. More than seven hundred guests came dressed as everyone from George Washington to Louis XV. Newspapers expressed outrage about their bills, which were in excess of $350,000, and the couple left America for a permanent vacation in England. But the ball was so memorable that the room's name was changed to the Bradley-Martin ballroom.

Fig. 12-4 View from East Thirty-third Street across Fifth Avenue to the brand new Waldorf Hotel, ca. 1893. This photograph shows the new, turreted hotel overshadowing the garden and home of Mrs. William B. Astor. Her home was demolished in 1897 for the Astoria Hotel. The two hotels were connected and became the city's most opulent hotel. It was later demolished to make way for the Empire State Building. Courtesy: Private Collection

Only a few years separated the Vanderbilts' taming of nature and the Astors' finding the avenue too noisy. So what had been a lazy rural road, fifty years earlier, ended the century as a brownstone-lined thoroughfare punctuated by church spires and chateaux. But Fifth Avenue was about to change . . . again.

1. *New York Times*, April 20, 1924.

2. Andrew Alpern and Seymour Durst, *HOLDOUTS!*, p. 102.

3. Moses King, *King's Handbook of New York City*, 1893, p. 402.

4. Moses King, *King's Handbook of New York City*, 1893, p. 696.

5. E. Idell Zeisloft, *The New Metropolis*, p. 162.

6. Moses King, *King's Handbook of New York City*, 1893, p. 354.

7. E. Idell Zeisloft, *The New Metropolis*, p. 274.

8. Robert B. King and Charles O. McLean, *The Vanderbilt Homes*, p. 30.

PART TWO

From Fortune to Fashion

A Blink in Time

The city restlessly swallowed everything in its path. Former suburbs and farmland were joined to the hub by subways, trains, and bridges. Telegraph and telephone systems brought everyone even closer. The city hummed with prosperity as buildings grew taller and automobiles whizzed through the streets.

The city tore down and built anew, passionately recreating itself every few years. Nothing in New York was permanent— neither buildings nor neighborhoods. Old-fashioned long before they became old, many buildings were considered to be fossils long before they deteriorated. The Waldorf-Astoria was less than ten years old before its luster was dimmed by the more

brilliant St. Regis; Morton Plant's home was less than fifteen years old before he left it for a more tranquil demesne.

Progress pushed ahead on the avenue. And every few years a writer would reminisce about Fifth Avenue's glorious past. The avenue was not a secure bastion despite the wealth of its residents. Unlike earlier downtown neighborhoods that gently declined into shabby gentility, residential Fifth Avenue just disappeared. Expensive homes, some occupied for just one generation, were quickly sold for commercial enterprises.

At the beginning of the century, the avenue was something like a stage set: Its marble monuments were minutes—but worlds—away from the city's boardinghouses, filth, and factories. Park Avenue's industry and tenements were just giving way to glamorous apartment buildings, and Sixth Avenue was squalid and dark beneath the tracks of the elevated trains. As late as 1909, two Texas steers escaped from abattoirs on First Avenue and eluded the desperate posse following them down Fifth Avenue. The avenue was lined with brownstones and grandiose mansions interspersed with pockets of trade and a few potential development sites, such as the property formerly occupied by the Roman Catholic Orphan Asylum and St. Luke's Hospital.

For a while, the avenue's languid nineteenth-century rhythm remained. On the village main street for millionaires, the affluent entertained at Sherry's, Delmonico's,

the St. Regis, or the Plaza. Men spent afternoons at the clubs while women went to the milliner or dressmaker. The privileged few even lived on the avenue. This was but a brief wink of time; Fifth Avenue was again in flux.

Patronized by wealthy neighbors, the Union Club and Sherry's did not immediately scare residents away to more fashionable areas. In 1901, "the general aspect of the avenue came more to resemble a Paris boulevard—minus the cafés—than any street to which New Yorkers were accustomed."[1] This intermingling of expensive homes with luxurious shops was temporary.

In the 1890s, the corners of Thirty-fourth Street and Fifth Avenue had been occupied by mansions. About ten years later a bank, a hotel, and a department store framed the portal to the grand thoroughfare. Jewelry stores and florist shops continued to move up the avenue in small increments. Before World War I, small specialty stores—Henri Bendel (1906), Bergdorf Goodman (1914), and Franklin Simon (1902)—appeared for the first time on the fashionable street. Large specialty stores such as Tiffany, Best & Co., and Bonwit Teller moved to their penultimate locations. For the most part, department stores moved to the avenue and stayed at one site: B. Altman, Lord & Taylor, and Arnold Constable clustered between Thirty-fourth and Forty-second streets, at the western edge of still-fashionable Murray Hill.

In the first twenty years of the

century, the seeds that had earlier been planted for Fifth Avenue's transformation started to flower into a version of today's thoroughfare. Stores offering medium priced merchandise, from women's clothing to pianos, and department stores offering nearly everything were located south of Forty-second Street to Thirty-fourth Street, and on to Herald Square. Office and loft buildings with ground floor shops in the middle Forties extended the Grand Central Terminal business district. Posh specialty shops and expensive hotels south of Central Park abutted the even more exclusive residential reaches north of Fifty-ninth Street.

The stores dislodged residences and within a few years, only a couple of homes remained below Forty-second Street. Simultaneous with this commercial trend on the southern end, specialty shops like Cartier joined exclusive hotels near Central Park. Since Madison Avenue and Fifty-seventh Street had not yet become fully established as posh shopping streets, Fifth Avenue offered everything from the most perfect diamonds to the most valuable Old Master paintings. And wealthy New Yorkers living near the Vanderbilt Colony were increasingly dismayed by trade's encroachment from both ends.

Starting as a gentle splash, trade became a wave that washed over the avenue leaving only a few random residents. By World War I, trade had won. Some stalwart residents remained on the avenue like Edith Wharton characters holding on to once-fashionable houses and neighborhoods. For these holdouts it was only a matter of time before they succumbed to either the disgrace of being surrounded by trade or the fiscal rewards of selling to trade. As business gained a foothold, the real estate prices escalated. So residents moved farther uptown and sold or leased their buildings for business purposes.

The patrician enclave became like a scene we recognize from a Childe Hassam painting of crowds and flags hung from large white buildings. The city's richest residents found themselves living on an avenue increasingly accessible to everyone: Pennsylvania Station opened in 1910, and Grand Central Terminal opened in 1913. There were Forty-second Street subway stations on the east and west sides, a Thirty-eighth Street station on the Sixth Avenue El, and the tantalizing possibility of linking the east and west side subways.

The Approach of Industry

Genteel trade establishments cemented their hold on the avenue. But the deluxe shops were trailed by garment factories. The Ladies Mile (Broadway) and Fashion Row (Sixth Avenue) were losing their cachet as nearby areas became crammed with lofts. Some factories moved uptown from the area we now call Soho; others were new enterprises. Garment factories filled the loft buildings springing up between Madison Square and the Waldorf-Astoria Hotel. Today, many of these loft buildings remain, their walls covered with faded advertisements.

Although writers had bemoaned trade, everyone thought the factory incursion was an absolute tragedy for the city. Society was so stratified that reputable journalists dismissed this incursion as an "infection" (as some called it) because the workers were not the "right" sort of people who should be crowding the avenue. The *New York Times* explained: "The fact that these loft buildings are being turned into manufacturing establishments is not a menace in itself, it is that they employ countless thousands of workers, and these congregate in front of the stores, especially during the noon hour, and so absolutely block the show windows."[2]

The Fifth Avenue Association

Alarmed at this factory encroachment, merchants, property owners, and hotel proprietors met at the Fifth Avenue Hotel in 1907 and founded the Fifth Avenue Association. The group intended to preserve the avenue's high standards and "oppose the wrong kind of commercialism. . . ." The founders included: Roland Knoedler, Simon Brentano, William Knabe, and Douglas L. Elliman. Robert Grier

Cooke, a rare book dealer, was president from 1908 until his death in 1924. By the summer of 1908, thirty-seven members paid annual dues of $10 apiece. In January 1909, they rented an office at 542 Fifth Avenue.

William M. Kendall, of McKim, Mead & White, wrote to Manhattan Borough President George McAneny in 1911 that, "This committee is concerned chiefly with the beauty of the avenue as a whole, rather than the beauty of each particular building. . . . The development of Fifth Avenue along the lines of beauty is largely a matter of the willingness of the architect and owner to sacrifice their own interests for the benefit of the whole . . . nothing could be worse at present than the section of the avenue from Twenty-third Street on—a jumble of buildings of greatly varying height and greatly varying color, without . . . consideration of the neighboring construction."

Gently stemming the flow of factories was impossible, so the Association began an all-out assault. Some members, allied with merchants, began the "Save New York" committee, and tried to enlist all New Yorkers to preserve the elite street. They first approached the problem by attacking the tall buildings. The group believed that if tall buildings blocked the light and air from neighboring residents, everyone's real estate values would be destroyed because mansions and clubs would abandon the avenue.

In 1911, the chairman of the association's Committee on Sanitation and Nuisances said that the avenue could "become an Eighth or Ninth Avenue, and ultimately even a First or Second Avenue . . . . If the present tendency toward scraping the sky continues, we may yet live to see the seemingly absurd spectacle of men groping their way with lanterns each afternoon at the bottom of deep canyons that were once Nassau and Wall Street."[3]

The association's opposition to the garment industry at its doorstep was one of the major thrusts behind the creation of portions of the 1916 Zoning Resolution. The association opposed factories above ground floor retail uses and supported height limits, believing that shorter buildings would prove economically unfeasible for manufacturing.

The 1916 Zoning Resolution, the first in the country, designated uses, heights and open space. Districts which permitted all uses, including factories, were mapped on Fifth Avenue south of Twenty-third Street; manufacturing was prohibited north of Twenty-third Street. The Zoning Resolution also established districts which were based on the relationship between street width and building height. Fifth Avenue, between Thirty-fourth and Fifty-eighth streets, was placed in a "one-and-a-quarter" height district, the lowest in midtown Manhattan. Buildings could be constructed to a height of one-and-a-quarter times the width of the street. The Grand Central Terminal area was in a "two" district, as was Fifth Avenue south of Thirty-fourth Street.

The height, setback, and tower regulations (which allowed a tower to be built on up to 25 percent of the lot area), encouraged buildings with setbacks, known as the "wedding cake" form. But Fifth Avenue would wait until the 1920s to see the results.

Once the garment industry had been pushed westward, the Association continued to work to protect the thoroughfare's beauty. In its commemorative book, *Fifty Years on Fifth*, the Association noted, "Nothing that draws a sidewalk crowd is considered good form." On one hand, they worked to eliminate unsightly people: "loiterers, newsboys, pedlars [sic], and other objectionable people from Fifth Avenue . . ."[4] But more than that, they have been scrupulously careful about monitoring anything that would weaken the strength of the city's premier retail street. Consistently they have opposed electric and protruding signs and bogus "going out of business" signs, and unfair business practices, such as linen stores that substituted cheaper cotton. After the zoning was enacted, the Save New York Committee convinced avenue manufacturers that their goods would not be sold on the avenue. By 1917, the committee claimed that the only manufacturers remaining on the avenue were those whose leases were not due to expire until the following year.

Although we may wince at the original ethnic overtones of keeping the immigrant workers off the avenue, one

could also argue that the result has been worth it. In 1917, the association began to give architectural awards in several categories, including best new building and best renovation.

Parades

Fifth Avenue—uptown or downtown—has always been the choice parade route. It has witnessed processions from every ethnic and religious group, fraternal organizations, unions, suffragettes, antisuffragists, and veterans (fig.16-1). In 1914, the city curbed parades and limited them (except for the traditional ones) to nonbusiness times. Many Fifth Avenue Association members

were delighted because they believed that parades harmed business.

At the turn of the century, parades were major events. On September 30, 1899, Admiral George Dewey, the victor of Manila Bay, was honored by a procession. When his carriage arrived at the Madison Square reviewing stand, the admiral got out. For four hours he stood and acknowledged the salutes of veterans of the Spanish-American War, the Union and Confederate armies, sailors, the National Guard and innumerable others.

For two weeks in October 1909, the city was taken over by the Hudson-Fulton celebration. The Fifth Avenue parade

Fig. 16-3 Designer Tom Lee sits behind models of the floats he designed for Fifth Avenue's 1957 Torchlight Parade. The floats ran the gamut from old-fashioned buses displaying 1907 fashions to a stairway holding famous "personality" Elsa Maxwell surrounded by bejeweled models. (See next photograph for actual float.) Courtesy: Collection of Sarah Tomerlin Lee

Opposite
Fig. 16-1 View north from West Forty-eighth Street during the Easter Sunday Parade, 1918. World War I is not yet over as the avenue is draped with wartime banners and the open-topped double-decked buses are covered with signs. Soldiers walk in the crowd of top-hatted men and well-dressed women. Note the single horse-drawn vehicle. Courtesy: Fifth Avenue Association

Fig. 16-2 This postcard shows B. Altman & Co. building during World War I when Fifth Avenue was the Avenue of the Allies. During a Red Cross drive, the store allowed groups of Red Cross nurses to exercise on its roof. Courtesy: Private Collection

Fig. 16-4 Models waving on Tom Lee's Telephone Company float at the 1957 Torchlight Parade. Courtesy: Collection of Sarah Tomerlin Lee

Fig. 16-5 View shows a World War II Bond Rally on Fifth Avenue. Of the long list of stores offering bonds and stamps, only five remain open. Courtesy: Lord & Taylor

featured floats representing historical events of the previous four hundred years and flags and groups from every nation that went into the "melting pot." Floats depicted everything from Pocahantas to tea being dumped into Boston Harbor to scenes from the Mexican-American War.

After years of Columbus Day parades, the day became a state holiday in 1909. To show gratitude to the Republicans for getting the holiday bill passed, a Republican Party leader (who happened to be Irish) was selected as the Grand Marshal. In desperation, a renegade group selected an Italian leader, and mapped out an alternate route up First Avenue. That year,

many people boycotted both, after huge parades in the past. Less than twelve thousand men marched along the Fifth Avenue route from south of Washington Square up to Fifty-eighth Street. As the marchers turned west on Fifty-eighth Street, they walked into an anti-Irish faction and both sides came to blows.

In 1918 the avenue was designated "Avenue of the Allies," as a backdrop for a solemn procession familiar to us from paintings of Childe Hassam (fig.16-2).

But those were the days of parades. The annual Police Parade, from the Battery to Fifth Avenue and Sixty-third Street, was once headed by Mayor Jimmy Walker. The

rather unhealthy-looking mayor paused a few times along the way for a cigarette, and ran up the stairs of St. Patrick's Cathedral to kneel and kiss the ring of Cardinal Hayes. From the sacred, he shortly headed a parade rather profane—the Beer Parade. The paraders called for the return of legal beer. The rationale for the parade was an economic one—the brew could be taxed to help the treasury. People from every neighborhood and every job—from the Hod Carriers Union to the Veterans of Foreign Wars—marched in the entertaining parade.

The avenue even celebrated itself in its 1957 "Torchlight Parade," sponsored by the Fifth Avenue Association. Its fifty years as a commercial thoroughfare was saluted by beautiful models and famous personalities riding on floats created and designed by designer Tom Lee, a man who spent most of his adult life beautifying Fifth Avenue (figs.16-3,16-4).

Even the avenue's war bond rallies were stylish. In one instance, Miss Dorothy Shaver had the glass removed from a Lord & Taylor window and addressed the crowds gathered on the avenue (fig.16-5).

Commerce

By 1908, writers reported that the "billionaire district" where residential palaces faced Central Park would become New York's version of London's fashionable Mayfair. However, many residents remained south of Fifty-ninth Street and battled the trade invasion. The Vanderbilts opposed apartment houses; the Fifth Avenue Presbyterian Church fought hotel bars. Then joining with the Fifth Avenue Association, they opposed trade in tall buildings.

The avenue's residential days were numbered. Just after the first commercial palaces were constructed, *Architectural Record* reported that the city's most radical changes had taken place on "the New Fifth Avenue" (between Twenty-sixth and Fiftieth streets) resulting in increased real estate values, carriage and pedestrian traffic. "It is, indeed, the only American street devoted for over a mile of its length exclusively to retail trade of a high class which has taken on a specific character. It has none of the air of quiet exclusiveness which characterizes Bond Street in London or the Rue de la Paix in Paris . . . [The Avenue] provides . . . exclusiveness . . . for the masses, and the wonder is that the masses can pay the price. One gets the impression on Fifth Avenue that all the world is there, that all the world has more money than it needs, and all the world rather likes to exhibit its superfluity."[5] So it's really a wonder that some of the city's wealthiest citizens stayed at all.

In the early years of the century the lower floors of brownstones were filled with dressmakers, mens' tailors, milliners, art and antiques dealers, and interior decorators. By relying on wealthy customers who often shopped by appointment, these shops were discreet enough to coexist with residential neighbors. The overall look of the avenue changed little. Some mansions were adapted for commercial use, but there were few major commercial buildings except for the Waldorf-Astoria and the Windsor Arcade between East Forty-sixth and Forty-seventh streets. Retailers considered the west side of the avenue preferable to the east side. Closer to bustling Broadway and Sixth Avenue, it was shadier in the afternoons and commanded higher rents. Real estate developer Seymour Durst remembers that even into the 1930s, from his office on Thirty-fourth Street he could see that, "Except for Altman's, the east side wasn't the 'right' side. We figured that only out-of-towners bought property on the east side."

With real estate prices on the rise, many homes were leased, not sold, for commercial purposes. The street had the intimate scale of, say, Madison Avenue.

Brownstone facades became frames for transparent screens of glass. With most of the lower stories replaced by large shop windows, the large expanse of glass provided a store's single source of light while serving as advertisement. Critics despaired that this made buildings look as if they rested "on a basement of glass." An architectural critic was furious about these "mutilated" brownstones, because they had become "apparition[s] of what [were] orderly and well designed dwelling house[s]..." He scoffed that little effort was made to improve the architectural beauty of the street by these "hybrid buildings that are called 'business premises.'"[6] Many of the side streets still have examples of these early conversions.

These alterations were the first step toward converting the avenue to one filled with stores. An uptown stroll would have revealed many store signs and the occasional tall, narrow building replacing a mansion. Certain sites, like those across from the Croton Reservoir, seemed better suited for commercial rather than residential use. In 1901-02, after the reservoir site was vacated in preparation for the New York Public Library, Edward M. Knox demolished the Lawrence Kip home across West Fortieth Street. On the site he erected the ten-story Knox Building (fig.17-1).

Knox, a Civil War hero, hired John Duncan, a prominent New York architect who had designed Brooklyn's Soldiers and Sailors Memorial Arch at Grand Army Plaza and Manhattan's Grant's Tomb at Riverside Drive and 122nd Street. Duncan designed this narrow commercial building in the Beaux-Arts style, a historical and rather eclectic style often used for residential and public buildings. But for its height, it could have been a mansion.

The rusticated limestone facade rises to an oversized cornice carried on console brackets above the sixth floor.

Overleaf page Fig. 17-1 View south from Forty-first Street, ca. 1925. The tallest point in this photograph is the scaffolded spire of the Brick Presbyterian Church. The 1902 Knox Building at the corner of Fortieth Street is the only structure on that block that still stands. The Avedon Building is next to the walled-in side yard of the Wendel House. Lord & Taylor and Franklin Simon can be viewed in the distance. Note traffic policemen at each corner and the bronze traffic tower at Thirty-fourth Street. Courtesy: Cushman & Wakefield

Above the eighth floor rises the two- story mansard roof pierced by one- and two-story dormer windows. Motifs of eagles, female heads, and palm branches punctuate the design, which is surmounted by elaborate cresting.

Produced in a factory at the corner of St. Marks and Grand avenues in Brooklyn, Knox hats were for sale on the first floor and mezzanine. The store kept conforms (head shapes) for many notable hat wearers: Enrico Caruso, Franklin D. Roosevelt, Al Smith, and John D. Rockefeller. The building's upper floors were used for executive offices for Knox and rented to other firms. Knox retained ownership of the Knox Building until his death in 1916. This designated New York City Landmark was converted for use as the headquarters of the Republic National Bank in 1964, and has subsequently been incorporated into the bank's new building.

In 1902, the thirty-seven-year-old Franklin Simon opened his women's specialty shop at Thirty-eighth Street and Fifth Avenue, on the site of Mrs. Marshall Orme Wilson's home. Wilson, the eldest son of Southerner Robert Wilson, had married Carrie Astor, the daughter of Caroline (*the* Mrs.) Astor. Simon, always proud of his early appearance on the avenue, displayed the store's logo with "Established 1902" on all display windows. The store lost $40,000 the first year and $28,000 the second; by the third, the firm was in the black for $16,000.

The son of a cigar maker, Simon had

left school at age thirteen to work for Stern Brothers where he arranged wholesale merchandise sent to the store to be evaluated by buyers. By age sixteen, he had been promoted to a buyer position. Stern's had allowed him two nights off a week to continue his education; after he established his business he started two scholarships for his employees at New York University's School of Retailing. He gave special discounts to nurses, clergymen, and civil-service employees.

Simon used to walk to work from 570 Park Avenue, and greeted many of his employees by name. He had said, "There is one principle that every merchant would do well to remember, and that is that his business is wholly dependent on public favor. He should do everything in his power to cater to the public, not only in the matter of merchandise but in any other way that will help build up good will. . . . Happy and satisfied employees are the best asset any house can have . . ."[7]

In 1904, the Singer Sewing Machine Company opened a store at 396 Fifth Avenue, a converted mansion next door to DePinna (which moved north in 1911). There it remained, little changed over the years, even after its executive offices moved to 30 Rockefeller Plaza.

This melange of buildings meant that the avenue didn't look like the Ladies Mile, with its imposing, cast-iron

Fig. 18-1 View north from West Thirty-fifth Street of east side of the avenue. The gleaming white marble Tiffany & Co. building stands out among residential brownstones and homes converted to shops.
Courtesy: Private Collection

department stores that lined and defined commercial streets. But when grandeur came to the avenue, its opulence was much greater than anything seen previously. Within a couple of years, small, circumspect shops were supplanted by elegant marble buildings modeled on ancient and Renaissance edifices. New York's finest architects designed these palaces—as glorious paeans to commerce, to money, to respectability. Their presence signaled the real change on the avenue. Fifth Avenue was going to be spectacular, in a tasteful sort of way.

McKim, Mead & White designed an imposing classical temple at the northwest corner of Thirty-fourth Street, across from the Waldorf-Astoria. The site had been occupied by A. T. Stewart's mansion converted into the Manhattan Club. It had been sold for sixty dollars a square foot for the Knickerbocker Trust Company's marble four-story building. The 1903 building must have looked like a very secure place in which to put money; the four Corinthian columns of Cippolino marble each weighed seventeen tons. The safe deposit vaults contained two thousand boxes behind doors weighing nine tons apiece, with hinges alone weighing 3,750 pounds. In 1921,

twelve floors were added and it became the Columbia Trust Building, with offices on the upper floors. The building stands today, but it has been altered beyond recognition.

Tiffany & Co. and Gorham

When large retail buildings were constructed serially, namely McKim, Mead & White's 1903-06 Tiffany & Co. and 1905 Gorham buildings, critics delighted in "the new Fifth Avenue. It is these buildings which linger in the minds of visitors to New York, and constitute a sort of selected and glorified vision of the thoroughfare, as the most remarkable and interesting business street in this country. . . . They are sumptuous, showy, and somewhat overwrought, but a genuine desire for architectural excellence has entered into their design and dignifies their pretensions."[8]

These stores were designed to be gracious neighbors to the nearby mansions. By using a residential vocabulary on a grand scale, the commercial palazzi bridged the change from residential to commercial. In the language of marble, these buildings spoke of luxury and respectability.

Tiffany & Co.'s white marble building at the southeast corner of Thirty-seventh Street (fig.18-1) (extant, ground-

floor alterations) was far more imposing than its cast-iron building on Union Square.

McKim, Mead & White's design was modeled on the sixteenth century Venetian Palazzo Grimani by Sanmicheli. The monumental scale of the seven-story building belied its height—it appeared to be a huge three-story building (fig.18-2). Three horizontal levels of double-height paired Corinthian columns and piers were surmounted by a hipped roof hiding an attic story.

The firm's figure of Atlas bearing a clock on his shoulders stood above the third floor. Atlas had embellished the firm's facade at 550 Broadway, and every facade thereafter. It almost served as the building's nameplate; Tiffany was one of the few stores not to have one.

A graduated set of steps that followed the avenue's contour led to Fifth avenue's five-bay facade. The three central bays were filled with display windows. The two end bays served as main entrances and led to a spacious selling floor, considered by many to be a museum of art objects. In a way it was High Society's department store, offering everything from engraved stationery and invitations to porcelain, art pottery, and silverware. In addition to precious objects like diamonds and oriental pearl necklaces, the store offered reasonably priced items, like watchchains and studs.

On Gorham's opening day in 1905, visitors pronounced it one of the city's "most artistic buildings" (fig.18-3) (extant, ground-floor

Fig. 18-4 View north from East Thirty-fifth Street of west side of the avenue, ca. 1908. The fashionable furrier, Jaekel, has moved next door to Gorham. Courtesy: Private Collection

alterations). They entered through the two-story Ionic arcade of gold-flaked granite. Between the arches were spandrels filled with figures in low relief representing arts and industries. All of the exterior bronze ornamentation as well as the bronze frieze above the first floor were cast at the company's foundry. The eight-story Indiana limestone building culminated in double-

Opposite
Fig. 18-3 View from East Thirty-sixth Street of the Gorham Building, ca. 1904. This photograph was taken before the store's grand opening in 1905. Except for Mrs. Louis Hoyt's brownstone mansion across Thirty-sixth Street, all of the nearby homes have been converted to shops. The three brownstones at the West Thirty-fifth Street corner were on the future site of Best & Co. Photo: Frank M. Ingalls. Courtesy: The New-York Historical Society, New York City

height engaged Corinthian columns supporting an entablature surmounted by Fifth Avenue's deepest and most extraordinary cornice.

Visitors were excited by the contents—$2.5 million worth of silver and gold. Sterling silver and fourteen-carat gold tableware were displayed on the first floor. Loving cups and dinner sets, stationery, and stained glass windows were on the upper floors. The ecclesiastical department was a room fitted out as a chapel.

Tiffany & Co. and Gorham were much larger than any of the other stores in the vicinity (fig. 18-4). However, as carriage trade operations, they offered wares expensive and exclusive enough to attract limited clienteles.

Department Stores on Fifth Avenue

B. Altman

The pace of the carriage trade's gentle march uptown had quickened when Benjamin Altman dipped his toe into the refined waters of Fifth Avenue. In 1904 he announced that his new department store would be constructed on the avenue. He and his store were known for high standards, but the store's very breadth of merchandise (ready-to-wear, home furnishings, and dry goods) meant that it would need to appeal to vast numbers of people. Although many of the small shops on this part of the avenue were not exclusive, none of them attracted large crowds.

Altman's announcement was not a complete surprise, because he had assembled land over the previous eight years from families such as Delano, Beekman, and Astor between Thirty-fourth and Thirty-fifth streets. And when property owners got wind of his identity, he was charged Fifth Avenue prices for properties on the side streets.

With Altman's announcement, a writer predicted that Fifth Avenue "will be gay and crowded and yet at the same time distinguished. Broadway was and is crowded; but it was always too miscellaneous to be distinguished. Fifth

Avenue is consistent and it is fashionable. It will contain nothing but hotels and shops—the most expensive in the city. . . . These buildings are designed by the best architects in the city, and will, when they become sufficiently numerous, give the avenue a very different atmosphere. Its architecture will be showy and so far unbusinesslike; but it will be adapted to fashionable stores, patronized by wealthy clients. It will be 'smart' and 'swell,' and will constitute an appropriate scenery for the panorama of the Fifth Avenue crowd."[9]

The normally staid B. Altman literally burst onto Fifth Avenue—even before the building was complete. Some thirty feet below the sidewalk during the foundation excavation, a construction worker drilled into rock which contained a forgotten charge of dynamite. Suddenly, an explosion scattered body parts of three dead construction workers along Madison Avenue. Many others, including Madison Avenue strollers, were seriously injured. Neighborhood windows were shattered and a fifty-pound stone fell through the roof of the rectory of the Church of the Incarnation and onto the bed of the just awakened sexton. Across Fifth Avenue, a Waldorf-Astoria

Previous page
Fig. 19-1 View from West Thirty-fourth Street shows B. Altman & Co, ca. 1907. The store building wraps around the corner brownstone occupied by M. Knoedler's art gallery. Residential brownstones along Thirty-fourth Street remain; the Madison Avenue frontage of the department store had not yet been built. Courtesy: KMO-361 Realty Associates/Mall Properties, Inc.

clerk reported that the explosion "caused no excitement" because the patrons were used to the constant noise from the excavation. Since this was a bit louder than usual, however, a few guests had gone to investigate.

Architects Trowbridge & Livingston designed an eight-story limestone version of a palazzo. Since Altman had been unable to purchase all of the property on the block, the store was constructed in phases which now appear seamless. The first section opened in 1906 with B. Altman in the entire Fifth Avenue frontage, except for the Thirty-fourth Street corner. That remained occupied by the converted brownstone of M. Knoedler and Co. (fig.19-1). After the gallery moved to 556 Fifth Avenue, B. Altman completed the corner section in 1911 (fig.19-2). The extension to Madison Avenue, which is twelve stories tall and somewhat more ornate, was completed in 1913 (fig.19-3).

Benjamin Altman did not live to get great enjoyment from his masterpiece. He died in 1913 at the age of seventy-three. (His funeral was at Temple Emanu-El.) By all accounts a reticent man, he was a beneficent employer. B. Altman's was among the first stores to close on Saturdays in the summer, have a school for employees, and a shorter business day. The resident of 626 Fifth Avenue (at West Fiftieth Street) had one other major interest: art. He traveled frequently to Europe to acquire art. He demolished a building behind his home to erect an art gallery. And, he left what was

then the largest bequest to the Metropolitan Museum of Art. His will created the Altman Foundation to oversee the store and promote the welfare of its employees. Mr. Altman was succeeded by Colonel Michael Friedsam, a relative and another art lover.

Altman made every architectural effort to be inoffensive to his residential neighbors. Stylistically, the avenue's first department store made sympathetic gestures to palazzo-like mansions. The building's monumental scale exudes respectability and grandeur (fig.19-4). Because of its sheer size and scale, it looked, both inside and out, like a museum. Since 1906, it has served as a weighty anchor, a boundary between riffraff and respectability.

In October 1906, the avenue's first department store opened without a nameplate. Ornamentation was minimal. Through the years architectural details such as column capitals and window surrounds have been removed, further simplifying an already severe design. Nearly human-sized pedestals support the monumental Ionic columns which form a two-story colonnade around the building. The main entrance is covered by a portico supported by elaborate columns. Display windows are set between the columns, above limestone bases that separate viewers from the view.

Opposite
Fig. 19-2 This photograph taken a few years later shows the Thirty-fourth Street corner under construction after M. Knoedler relocated to a site farther north. Courtesy: New York City Landmarks Preservation Commission, B. Altman archives

Surmounting these are semicircular windows which lend the appearance of one giant story. The square-headed windows of the third through sixth floors had molded surrounds. An architrave extends above the sixth story, below the double-height arched windows of the seventh and eighth floors. An entablature beneath a strong cornice decorated by lions' heads surmounts the building.

The store's interior was marvelously light and airy. With the magnificent rotunda rising above the 1906 building, broad aisles, high ceilings, and clusters of electric light bulbs, B. Altman offered a shopping experience like no other (fig.19-5, 19-6). Unlike European department stores which draped rugs and textiles over the balustrades, and walled off small departments, B. Altman kept the sprinklered floors open. But for the elaborately detailed rotunda and elevator doors, the fixtures and cases were fairly simple.

When the enlarged store opened in 1914, it issued a catalogue which described the serenity and calm that pervaded the store and continued almost to its last days. "[T]he attention is instantly riveted by the broad, airy spaces, the restful color scheme,

Previous page
Fig. 19-3 View of B. Altman building taken from the Empire State Building. After the last phase of construction in 1913, B. Altman encompassed the entire block. The Madison Avenue frontage was taller than that on Fifth Avenue. Note that B. Altman had not yet installed its name on the facade. Courtesy: KMO-361 Realty Associates/Mall Properties, Inc.

the pervasive atmosphere of refinement and dignity. It is characteristic of the Altman system, originated by Mr. Altman himself— who as an organizer had no superior—that, notwithstanding the tremendous volume of business transacted in the store every day in the year, there is everywhere apparent a certain poise, which conveys to the keen observer the mental impression of a great organization kept under perfect control—a gigantic piece of well-constructed, well-cared-for machinery of which every infinitesimal part is accurately placed and keyed." And yet, this Victorian artifact had a private generator. An electrical inspector employed by the city remembers that Altman's was one of the few buildings with electricity during the city's 1965 blackout.

As the construction of the Waldorf-Astoria fifteen years earlier had helped to launch Fifth Avenue's commercial course, the arrival of B. Altman did the same. Their sheer size precluded both tasteful establishments from exclusivity. Altman's daring move made a Fifth Avenue address a necessity for the other large stores. All of the early stores echoed Altman's efforts to defer to the avenue's respectability; the buildings were designed to be simple, almost severe, solid, and prosperous.

Within the large and substantial buildings, only the lower floors were used for retail sales. The upper floors were occupied by wholesaling operations and even garment manufacturing. Personal service was emphasized; customers weren't confronted

by rows of racks. Merchandise was displayed; salesclerks assisted customers by retrieving the articles stored behind the counters and in stockrooms. Even paying for merchandise was a labor-intensive activity. Money was placed in a pneumatic tube which was pumped to a cashier's office, where change was made and returned in a similar tube (fig.19-7). Gentlemen floorwalkers, some rising from the ranks of salesmen and others recently graduated from college, patrolled the aisles. They answered questions, took complaints, gave advice, and, in general, maintained calm.

Pleasant as these stores were for shoppers, they were also, relatively speaking, comfortable spaces in which to work. The larger stores provided their employees with services similar to those offered by contemporaneous settlement houses: classes, medical care, outings, and subsidized meals. Perhaps Lord & Taylor supplied the most elegant surroundings, but to some degree all the stores provided the same services. During World War I, the Consumers League of New York City listed all of the department and specialty stores with the number of weeks of paid vacations (usually one week after one year of service, going to two weeks, sometimes more, after two years). The mostly female salesclerks were required to wear dark colors, creating an almost uniform background for the fashionable shoppers.

By World War I, the avenue between Thirty-fourth and Forty-second

Fig. 19-4 This ca. 1980s view of B. Altman shows the stately building badly in need of cleaning. Photo: Carl Forster. Courtesy: New York City Landmarks Preservation Commission

Overleaf
Fig. 19-5 This view of B. Altman's rotunda underscores the beauty of details such as leaded glass, and filagreed work on the elevator doors and balcony railings. Mannequins are not yet used to model clothing, or, in this case, women's undergarments—these are exhibited on dressmakers' forms. Courtesy: KMO-361 Realty Associates/Mall Properties, Inc.

streets was concentrated with department stores. The small, exclusive shops found homes farther uptown.

Fifth Avenue became such an important retail address that McCreery's, a large store with entrances on Thirty-fourth and Thirty-fifth streets, purchased a sliver of the avenue—not much more than an entrance and a display window—for the important avenue address. (The store

Fig. 19-7 This photograph from B. Altman's catalog shows a view of the Pneumatic Tube Room filled with serious young male cashiers. Courtesy: Private Collection

Previous page
Fig. 19-6 View of B. Altman's rotunda, ca. 1907. The main floor offered an eclectic assortment of merchandise, including dress goods, linings and notions, ribbons, men's furnishings, and cameras. Children's wear is visible on the second floor. The store's emphasis on personal service is apparent as the display counters are bordered by built-in seating, and very little merchandise is actually within reach of the customer. The interior was far more spacious than those of the later Fifth Avenue department stores. Courtesy: KMO-361 Realty Associates/Mall Properties, Inc.

closed in the 1950s; its Thirty-fourth Street building was then occupied by Ohrbach's which had moved from Fourteenth Street.)

Best & Co.

Moving from West Twenty-third Street, Best & Co. opened on the northwest corner of Thirty-fifth Street in 1910 (extant, alterations). The six-story building of Ohio stone was designed by Townsend, Steinle & Hackell. The simply ornamented facade with sills, lintels, and a balustrade above the cornice looked like an elegant apartment house.

Best & Co.'s Lilliputian Bazaar had been the only store in the city to specialize in children's clothing. It designed and manufactured many of its clothes. In this larger building, it expanded to women's clothing and accessories. The first three floors used were finished in mahogany, with

Opposite
Fig. 19-8 View north of west side of the avenue between Thirty-sixth and Thirty-seventh streets, ca. late 1970s. The building at the Thirty-seventh Street corner was designed by Warren and Wetmore and contained Stewart & Co. and Mark Cross on the lower floors. The building occupied by Maison Chic had held the store for Singer sewing machines. The small building on its left had been the first DePinna. Courtesy: New York City Department of City Planning

19-8

61

broad aisles, "affording ample room for a large number of customers at the various counters without excessive crowding."[10]

Real estate prices on the avenue continued to climb, escalating even monthly. In 1907, a developer purchased a single lot on Thirty-eighth Street directly across the street from Franklin Simon. At a bit less than the asking price of $700,000, he paid $277 a square foot, a higher price than for property in the financial district.

This lot became part of the parcel that Bonwit Teller & Company moved to in 1910 from West Twenty-third Street. The store occupied the lower floors of a new ten-story office building at 417 Fifth Avenue (extant, ground-floor alterations). Designed by Buchman & Fox, the brick and stone building was altered and enlarged five years later by Howells and Stokes.

On property his family owned on the southwest corner of West Thirty-seventh Street, across from Tiffany, Robert W. Goelet demolished the building occupied by the china and glass firm of Davis Collamore. He hired Warren and Wetmore to design a building in 1914 for Stewart and Company, a new women's specialty shop (extant, ground-floor alterations) (fig.19-8).

Stewart and Company occupied the first two floors of the eight-story building. The firm stayed until 1928, when it moved uptown for a short period. The upper floors have large windows framed by delicately detailed terra cotta painted white and blue. It is now popularly known as the Wedgwood Building for its resemblance to the

pottery.[11]

In 1914, Mark Cross moved from Twenty-sixth Street to Thirty-seventh Street (fig.19-9). The company had been founded in Boston by Henry W. Cross and his son, Mark. Upon the death of Mark Cross, the company was inherited by Patrick Francis Murphy, who had begun as a seventeen-year-old apprentice. Murphy is now better known as the father of Gerald Murphy, painter, host, and bon vivant friend of F. Scott Fitzgerald.

The elder Murphy had built up the company; the younger Murphy continued to modernize its lines and, for instance, looked to superbly wrought motoring accessories to replace more traditional harness and saddle products. For the first time, luxury items were covered in traditional English leathers as the store imported golf clubs, thermos bottles, and cigarette cases. In 1916, Mark Cross sold the first wristwatch in America. The store remained there until 1935. It moved several times thereafter, to Fifty-second Street, Fifty-fifth Street, and now is in the Olympic Tower building.

Architect Harry Allen Jacobs designed a store and showroom for the Hardman Peck Piano Company at 433 Fifth Avenue (extant, ground-floor alterations) (fig.19-10). But for the ground floor display windows, the 1911 marble facade looked like a delicately scaled residential palazzo.

The ground floor was complimented for its large curtained display window and putti-filled panel above

the entrance. Above this was the facade's focal point: a triple arcade supported by slender columns in front of deeply recessed windows. The fifth floor's windows were flanked by panels of musical attributes; the projecting cornice and balustrade cast the upper facade in deep shadow.

The store's interior continued the residential ambiance, displaying pianos in homelike environments. Each room was designed differently—as large or small living rooms, or even as a paneled stateroom of a yacht.

Benson and Hedges had a shop next door; at the southeast corner of Thirty-ninth Street was an eleven-story building with double-height display windows erected for Knabe Pianos (extant, ground-floor alterations) (fig.19-11). The upper floors were used for offices, shops, and showrooms.

Lord & Taylor

By purchasing the northwest corner of Thirty-eighth Street, the Burton brothers were about to realize a dream. Years before, their father had owned the entire avenue frontage. He sold it all, except for his home. As Fifth Avenue prospered, he (and later his sons) attempted to buy back their former property. J. H. Burton was asked how it felt to pay $925,000 for property his father had sold forty years before for $47,000. He replied,"Well, if you've ever bagged anything after gunning

Fig. 19-9 This is a 1924 advertisement for the Mark Cross shop in the Stewart Building. Courtesy: Fifth Avenue Association

for it for twelve years, I think you have a fair idea of how we feel over getting that lot..."[12] With this purchase, they held one of the largest parcels under single ownership between Madison Square and Central Park. Quickly, newspapers were rife with rumors about department stores.

In 1914, Lord & Taylor opened its store on the Burton site. It had been founded at 47 Catherine Street in 1825 by Samuel Lord, an Englishman. Within a year, he enlarged the store and took his wife's cousin, George Washington Taylor, into partnership. The store gradually moved uptown, until it erected a cast-iron building on Broadway and Twentieth Street in 1872. This building was enlarged several times; and in 1902 the store was extended to Fifth Avenue, so it can claim to be the first store on Fifth Avenue.

An estimated seventy-five thousand to one hundred thousand patrons entered Lord & Taylor's ten-story building during its 1914 "housewarming." The West Thirty-ninth Street corner continued to hold Black,

Fig. 19-10 Contemporary view of the former Hardman Peck Piano Building shows that most of the facade of this 1911 commercial palazzo remains intact except for the ground floor. Photo: Andrew Wist

Starr & Frost (since 1898) in a building owned by jeweler Michael Dreicer. The jewelry firm moved uptown and Vantines moved in. (Through the years, that building has held a number of tenants, including Ovington's, Jay Cobbs, and Doubleday Doran. Only recently has Lord & Taylor expanded into the building.)

Designed by Starrett and Van Vleck, the restrained Italian Renaissance adaptation had every modern convenience sheathed in deluxe materials and delicately wrought detail (fig.19-12). This was Fifth Avenue's first store that actually looked like a store, not a palace or a museum.

The two-story limestone base is punctured by the main, round arched entry on Fifth Avenue, the Thirty-eighth and Thirty-ninth street entrances, and the display windows. The midsection, of glazed gray brick, supports a two-story limestone pilaster screen surmounted by a copper cornice. The entrance vestibules were finished in Botticino marble and travertine with vaulted ceilings of Guastavino tile.

The Fifth Avenue show windows had backgrounds of Caen stone ornamented in the Adam style (fig.19-13).

The luxurious interior was fairly ornate but most of the finishes have been removed over the years. Buff travertine stone bordered at the aisle edges by black Egyptian gold-veined marble covered the main floor. The groin-vaulted ceilings were divided by arched ribs ornamented with panels and medallions in low relief. Walls and fixtures were of African mahogany. At

Fig. 19-11 View north from West Thirty-seventh Street, ca. 1909. The tall building occupied by Knabe Pianos at East Thirty-ninth Street looms over two homes. Just across the street from Knabe is the Union League clubhouse. The street clock in the foreground stood in front of Franklin Simon. Courtesy: Private Collection

the rear of the ground floor was the balcony mezzanine which displayed fresh flowers in refrigerators set into Rookwood pottery cases. Delicate Adam-style woodwork was used throughout the building, even on the walls of the upholstered passenger elevators. The "semi-indirect" lighting fixtures used glass designed for the building which eliminated yellow rays—resulting in pure white light. To resolve any lighting issues before installation, the architects had created a mock-up of four bays of the ground floor in the sixty-ninth Regiment Armory.

On opening day, guides conducted tours throughout the store to describe the conveniences and new and expanded departments. Retaining departments like the dress pattern department (fig.19-14), the store also offered more modern sections such as one devoted to "apparel and accessories for motoring" with a branch of the New Jersey Automobile license bureau issuing driver's licenses and license plates. The Equestrienne section sported a

Opposite
Fig. 19-12 This ca. 1950 view shows Fifth Avenue's first department store that was actually designed to look like a store. Its flowered awnings "announce Spring's arrival." Photo: Ben Greenhaus. Courtesy: Lord & Taylor

19-13

19-14

mechanical horse to ensure perfectly fitting riding habits. Lord & Taylor boasted that they would have a year-round toy department here. The large Fur Storage Vault was "a store feature which is original with Lord & Taylor and the last word in cold storage vault construction." The third floor held the "greatest ready-to-wear section in the world." The fourth-floor salon, with a "completely appointed Bijou stage" displayed imported fashions twice a year. The walls of the salon were paneled with a series of small display alcoves holding gowns and wraps.

The store offered a wide range of services including rooms in the mezzanine basement for suburban customers to change from afternoon to evening wear. (The store then delivered the clothes home free of charge.) The fifth-floor Studio of Interior Decoration frequently changed its decorative scheme.

Three restaurants were on the tenth floor: the Loggia, with windows which opened onto Fifth Avenue; the exotic Mandarin Room and the elegant Wedgwood Room, decorated in the Adam style with

chairs and tables from Thonet and Limoges china. The seven-piece orchestra that serenaded the diners could also be heard in the rooftop Employees Dining Room.

The employees were assigned to three lunch rooms—one for women and girls, the other for men and boys, and the third for workroom employees and those bringing their own lunch. The girls and boys employed as messengers ate subsidized lunches. The store provided a gym, dentist's office, and rooftop recreation space (still in use). Lord and Taylor asserted that "the entire energies of the institution have been concentrated on presenting to New York and the entire nation the greatest assortments of the world's finest merchandise at the lowest possible prices."

Within a short period, Lord & Taylor was in financial straits. In 1914, a committee of New York bankers, and Colonel Michael Friedsam (B. Altman vice-president), chose Arkansas banker Samuel W. Reyburn as treasurer.

Reyburn, who served as president from 1916–1936, closed Lord & Taylor's wholesale division, repaid the $5 million-plus owed to New York banks, and brought the store back into the black.

Arnold Constable

The last of the department stores to move uptown was Arnold Constable and Co. The store had been founded in 1825 at 91 Pine Street by Aaron Arnold, an Englishman.

James Constable, another Englishman, joined him in 1838 and married Arnold's daughter Henrietta in 1845. The store gradually moved uptown, to Marble House at Mercer, Howard, and Canal streets. Mrs. Abraham Lincoln was one of their customers there. Arnold Constable began to bill customers monthly, rather than biannually, as had been the practice in most of the stores. In 1869 the store moved to Nineteenth Street where it remained until 1914.

During its 1914 summer clearance sale of over one million dollars' worth of merchandise from its store on the Ladies Mile, Arnold Constable & Co. admitted that it was considering several uptown sites for a new home. Within several months, the store announced its purchase of Frederick W. Vanderbilt's house on the southeast corner of Fortieth Street, and the adjacent former George Morgan home on East Fortieth Street and its stable on Thirty-ninth Street. That sale left the Wendel residence as the only one remaining between Thirty-fourth and Forty-second streets.

Architect T. J. Bartley designed a simple six-story building (extant, ground-floor alterations) that wrapped around the Union League Club and had entrances on each street. The main entrance was on Fifth Avenue, the carriage entrance was on Fortieth Street, and a double entrance was on Thirty-ninth Street. The 1915 opening day crowd was greeted by the great-great granddaughter of Aaron Arnold and huge bouquets and wreaths sent by the city's other department stores.

The fittings decreased in luxuriousness as the elevation increased; the main floor was Circassian walnut; the second floor was mahogany, and the third floor was oak. The main floor offered "general merchandise," the second held women's clothing, and the third and fourth were for rugs and upholstery, with a portion reserved for executive offices. The fifth and sixth floors were occupied by wholesale departments. The store had the ubiquitous "Silk Room" with varied lights to test the colors of silks in different lights, including daylight. Adjoining the store on Fifth Avenue was a small two-story building constructed with footings and columns strong enough to carry additional stories to house "the famous $50,000 Arnold Constable Louis Quinze Salon," with wainscoting and chandeliers transferred from the Broadway store.

For a few years, Fifth Avenue was like a white, rich cream puff with a backdrop of new, gleaming white or ivory stores. But the sweetness of this confection was controlled. Stores were never open late and they closed on Saturdays in the summers. Chauffeurs, doormen, delivery boys, and servants smoothed the way for Madam. Uniformed doormen opened doors, assistants polished brass and kept the streets immaculate, liveried servants waited at carriage entrances for their mistresses (fig.19-15). Nothing jarring like neon or protruding signs spoiled the view. Show windows were crowded with deluxe clothing and accessories.

In December 1911, the Burton Brothers purchased a Kip house at 448 Fifth Avenue between Thirty-ninth and Fortieth Streets for $700,000 ($193 a square foot)—a record price for an interior lot. They were certain that the adjacent Wendel house and yard would remain and allow light and air onto their property for many years to come. To the north it abutted a converted town house and the Knox building on the Fortieth Street corner. Knox had purchased his corner site ten years before for approximately half the

Fig. 19-15 Early view shows B. Altman's carriage entrance on East Thirty-fifth Street. Courtesy: New York City Landmarks Preservation Commission, B. Altman archives

Opposite
Fig. 19-16 This rental advertisement for a Fifth Avenue store shows how window displays could be maximized for a narrow store. Courtesy: Cushman & Wakefield

FOR RENT
STORE, MEZZANINE & BASEMENT
Will Change Store Front as Shown Below, or Will Consider Changes as May Be Required by Tenant

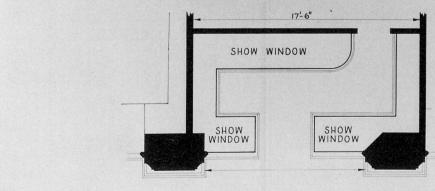

For particulars apply to Agent on Premises

price.

The Burton property had been the home of William V. Brady, New York's mayor in 1847–48. His daughter Cornelia had married Dr. Isaac Kip, one of the city's best known doctors, who died at age eighty-one in 1911. After a surveyor's error was discovered, the Burtons refused to close on the property. Years of litigation ensued. The Burtons won and the property reverted back to the Kip estate.

Its first floor was leased to Avedon & Co., a women's clothing store. In 1920, the building was demolished. Architect Harry Allen Jacobs designed a new building for Avedon which included an arcaded shopfront, possibly the first in New York City (demolished). This type of facade maximized display possibilities, particularly for stores with narrow avenue frontage. Behind the central entrance was a short passage lined with windows, which often lead to another vestibule lined with display windows. Shoppers could view a multitude of items while protected from crowds and weather (fig.19-16).

The New York Public Library

On the site of the Croton Reservoir, a structure revered and hated, rose the New York Public Library, a regal monument adored by everyone (fig. 20-1). Far shorter than any of the buildings near it and set back from the lot line, the library commands its site like a dignified and self-assured monarch.

The building is located on a terrace divided by a wide flight of steps guarded by stone lions sculpted by E. C. Potter. The white Vermont marble palace designed by Carrère and Hastings, has a central triple-arched portico from which extend wings surmounted by pediments. Six figures sculpted by Paul Bartlett stand against the attic above the entrance portico to separate the names of the three collections joined under the roof.

At the end of the nineteenth century, New York City had several marvelous research collections, but they were virtually inaccessible to the public because of limited hours. In 1895, the New York Public Library had been formed by consolidating three collections: the Trustees of the Astor Library, the Trustees of the Lenox Library, and the Tilden Trust. In 1901, the eleven branches of the New York Free Circulating Library joined.

The cornerstone of the New York Public Library was laid on November 10, 1902, and the building opened on May 23, 1911. Architect John Carrère was killed in an automobile accident shortly before the library opened, and his body lay in state in the Great Hall.

The magnificent library was eminently practical. Dr. John Billings, the library's first director, worked with the architects to achieve a superb research facility. For instance, the splendid reading room was placed on the third floor for maximum light, air, and quiet, and also easy access to the stacks of books beneath it. (From Bryant Park, the placement of the stacks is obvious from the narrow windows in the fairly severe western facade.)

Except for the (since relocated) Central Circulation Branch, the books could not be removed from the building. The library was open from 9:00 A.M. to 10:00 P.M. every day (and holidays) and from 1:00 P.M. to 10:00 P.M. on Sundays. Today's hours, unfortunately, are shorter. The library is closed Sundays and Mondays, but the building, continually restored and renovated, looks better than it

Fig. 20-1 One of the pair of E. C. Potter's beloved lions guards the library's main entrance. Photo: Casey Cronin. Courtesy: The New York Public Library

Fig. 20-2 This 1990 photograph shows the triple-arched entrance of the main library at Fifth Avenue and Forty-second Street. Photo: Casey Cronin. Courtesy: The New York Public Library

ever has.

Of course, the building is a designated New York City Landmark, and listed on the National Register of Historic Places. Much of the marble interior is a designated New York City interior landmark as well.

The majestic lobby gleams with white marble from floor to barrel-vaulted ceiling. From there, one can walk into the Gottesman Exhibition Hall or many of the smaller rooms located off the marble-lined corridors, including the lovely book shop which was originally the Library for the Blind.

Two grand staircases, on either side of the Astor Hall, lead eventually to the third floor. There, the central rotunda separates the Edna Barnes Salomon exhibition room from the catalogue room, which leads to the main reading rooms. With the soft lighting emanating from the bronze reading lamps, oak furniture, and high, arched windows, one becomes aware of the generations of readers, researchers, and writers who have spent hours, days, and months in focused attention and suspended animation.

A Wider Avenue

After the turn of the twentieth century, the avenue underwent a dramatic change—mainly because of complaints about traffic congestion. Mostly, the problems were caused by "unruly hansom cabs" and oil dropping from the brand-new automobile engines which made the street dangerous for horses and delivery vehicles.

Winter storms damaged the street and further hampered its normally slow-moving traffic. The avenue was impassable because of "sinkholes, ridges, and mudpiles that decorate the entire length of Fifth Avenue. . . . For many blocks scarcely a yard's length could be found that lacked its quota of holes in the asphalt, large or small, deep or shallow, with corresponding jolts and lurches."[13]

Vehicular problems were coupled with sidewalk encroachments, such as areaways, stoops, and sidewalk cafés. As the architecture became grander and the traffic increased, there were more complaints about the quality of the thoroughfare. Mark Cross, then located on Twenty-sixth Street, sued the adjacent restaurant because its "summer garden" (sidewalk café) blocked the sidewalk. After the leather goods shop won its case, the city took notice and started a few suits of its own to clear the avenue's sidewalks.

In 1903, the New York City Improvement Commission was created to develop a comprehensive plan for the city's development. A few years later, the mayor reported on the commission's recommendations, one of which was the widening of the Fifth Avenue roadway between Twenty-third and Fifty-ninth Streets. One of the many recommendations which never came to pass was submerging Forty-second Street eighteen feet beneath an overpass on the avenue.

Few of the commission recommendations were carried out quickly. But by 1909 Fifth Avenue underwent the first phase of its widening program.

On maps, Fifth Avenue was one hundred feet wide. Two thirty-foot-wide sidewalks flanked its forty-foot-wide roadway, which ostensibly provided room for four lanes of traffic. However, maps did not reflect reality on the two-way avenue. Vehicles waiting at the curbs allowed only one lane of traffic to pass each way. The sidewalks were congested with pedestrians navigating around encroachments that had been allowed temporarily by the Board of Aldermen, with the proviso that they were to be removed by property owners whenever use of the public street—as mapped—became necessary.

The city's plan was to add 15 feet to the roadway by pushing each curb back 7 1/2 feet: Since the sidewalks would thereby be reduced to 22 1/2 feet, property owners were to remove all encroachments with exceptions of up to 2 1/2 feet.

Between Twenty-fifth and Forty-seventh streets, steps, protruding shop windows and courtyards were required to be removed. Even subcellars (often extending thirty feet beneath the sidewalk) needed to be arched to support the new sidewalks and traffic. Brownstones lost both space and style as facades underwent major alterations. Wide flights of stairs leading to grand entries were replaced by a few meager steps. Tiffany lost a few steps. B. Altman escaped damage because removal of its columns—which extended four feet onto the sidewalk—would have required removal of the actual avenue facade.

When a Corporation Counsel staffmember called on Sherry's to investigate the status of the strengthening of the roof of its sidewalk vault, he was "informed in pained tones that the famous wine cellar . . . is under the area, and that the old dust-covered and cobwebby bottles are being tenderly transferred to another part of the cellar as rapidly as the importance of the occasion will allow. Even the heart of a city employe [sic] was touched by this plea, and he said no more."[14]

The New York Edison Company took advantage of the torn-up streets to install a new lighting system to replace the haphazardly arranged lamps (fig. 21-1).

The second phase of widening the avenue between Forty-seventh and Fifty-eighth Streets was approved in 1911. Despite the protests of a couple of property owners, notably the Fifth Avenue Presbyterian Church, the city went ahead.

This widening struck at the heart of high society—the city's finest residential and ecclesiastical properties suffered. Within a few months the avenue was a complete mess. A writer glumly reported, "A stranger might well think that house wreckers had taken possession of the eleven blocks . . . and were preparing to tear down several rows of fine brownstone mansions to replace them with towering business structures . . ."[15]

William K. Vanderbilt's house lost its broad flight of stone steps and areaway. Mrs. William D. Sloane's northern "twin" house lost its garden. Mrs. Russell Sage's home lost its high stoop; and the removal of its bay window on the parlor floor left a gaping hole for a time.

Cornelius Vanderbilt's chateau lost part of its wrought iron fence which had been custom made in France. A specially chartered tug boat hauled the pieces of the fence to sea so a junkman couldn't copy the design by reusing the salvage.

St. Patrick's Cathedral lost a high grassy bank and wide steps; the Collegiate Church at Forty-eighty Street lost its stone and iron railing. The St. Regis and Gotham hotels lost their raised summer gardens.

So, coupled with the avenue's changing uses and its new, grand architecture was the removal of the stoops and widening of the street. Shearing the stoops, steps, and gardens ended the visual rhythm typical of residential streets. Suddenly large stores appeared to be more at home than the homes. And the avenue gained the impressive look of a smart commercial boulevard.

Small Shops North of Forty-second Street

The character of the area around Forty-second Street changed quickly as residential buildings became commercial. Banks, albeit small and discreet, had been moving into the area since the 1870s. As hotels and office buildings were constructed near the new Grand Central Terminal, Forty-second Street became even more important. The pedestrian and vehicular traffic was quite heavy in this area. In 1903, Russell Sage moved from his home of forty years just north of Forty-second Street. The formerly genteel Hotel Bristol had been converted to stores and offices and Sage's rent tremendously escalated because of the area's trade potential. He felt that he could "hold out no longer against the encroachments of business . . ."[16] Yet the frame market, "Ye Olde Willow Cottage," stood into this century at the southeast corner of Forty-fourth Street.

In 1906, the Farmers' Loan and Trust Company opened a branch office at Forty-first Street and Fifth Avenue. It claimed to be the first of the downtown trust companies to move uptown. Boss Tweed's home, 511 Fifth Avenue at the southeast corner of Forty-third Street, was demolished for the sixteen-story Postal Life Building (extant, ground-floor alterations). In 1917, the York and Sawyer design won the Fifth Avenue Association's gold medal for new construction.

With large stores clustering below Forty-second Street (and Stern Brothers actually opening on West Forty-second Street), specialty shops such as jewelry stores, tastefully dressed as small gems, continued to be constructed in the Forties (fig.22-1). Henri Bendel opened his specialty shop in a converted town house at 520 Fifth Avenue in 1906.

Warren and Wetmore's 1907 building for the jeweler Dreicer & Co. which moved from 292 Fifth Avenue to 560 Fifth Avenue at Forty-sixth Street, (extant, altered) was considered "a more beautiful study in grace and refinement than any building of its sort in the city."[17] The delicately detailed building conveyed an air of French luxe and refinement. The ground floor's black "Porte d'Or" marble (black and gold) and columns were highlighted by dull gilded bronze capitals and bases. Above this a stringcourse supported paired pilasters which rose to the main cornice. It was surmounted by an iron railing in front of the recessed attic story (fig. 22-2).

Its showrooms were designed with period decoration as appropriately sumptuous backgrounds for jewels and precious objects. Dreicer & Co. adapted Louis XV commod es and tables to hold objects on display, so that the store had the intimate ambiance of a French town house. When Michael Dreicer died in 1921, he left a grand bequest to the Metropolitan Museum of Art. A final sale was held; the

Fig. 22-1 Easter Sunday view looking north from Forty-fourth Street. Exclusive shops were still clustered in this area in stores designed by the city's premier architects. Starting at the West Forty-fifth Street corner are: Alice Maynard, Andrew Alexander Shoes, Hollander, M. Knoedler, and Dreicer. Across Forty-sixth Street is Thorley's House of Flowers. Courtesy: Fifth Avenue Association

Previous page Fig. 21-1 View north from Forty-second Street taken June 26, 1923. Alfred Dunhill and Sulka are neighbors on the west side of the avenue and the Columbia Bank in the Postal Life Building and Temple Emanu-El are across East Forty-third Street from each other. Photo: Standard Photographic Service. Courtesy: Fifth Avenue Association

store did not last much longer.

Selling the northeast corner of Thirty-fourth Street to B. Altman, M. Knoedler & Co. moved to 556–558 Fifth Avenue in 1912 on the former site of the Lotos Club. Of Chasignelles limestone

imported from France, the four-story building was designed by Carrère and Hastings. Modeled on an Italian Renaissance palazzo, the rusticated base held three monumental arches. The central entrance, flanked by display windows, led

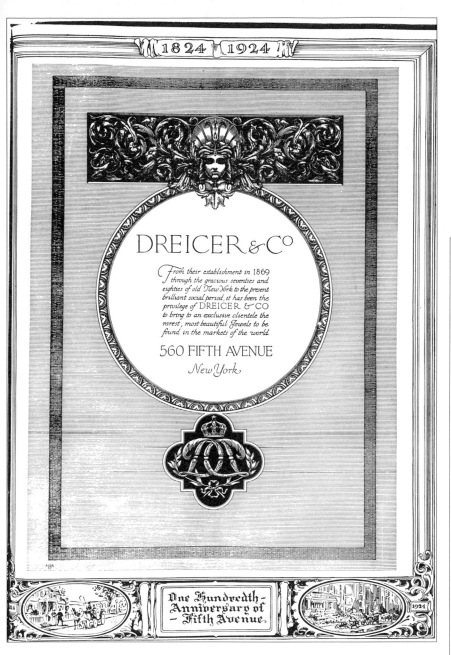

Fig. 22-2 This advertisement comes from a 1924 commemorative book about Fifth Avenue. Courtesy: Fifth Avenue Association

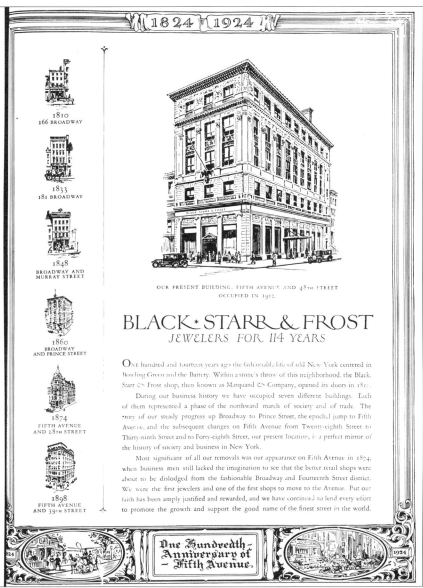

Fig. 22-3 This advertisement from the 1924 commemorative book about Fifth Avenue shows Carrère & Hastings' beautiful design, now obliterated. In 1912, Black, Starr & Frost had moved into this building from the one adjacent to Lord & Taylor. Courtesy: Fifth Avenue Association

Fig. 22-4 Behind the newly restored and landmarked facades is Henri Bendel's flagship store and an office tower. The pristine Lalique windows of the Coty Building are now visible from the street and are an integral part of Henri Bendel's superb store design. Courtesy: Henri Bendel

through a small vestibule to a large columniated reception hall which opened onto three galleries of different sizes.

After the gallery moved to the Upper East Side, the palazzo was occupied by Schrafft's, one of a restaurant chain with moderately priced food. The restaurant, famous for its ice-cream sodas and an atmosphere of faded gentility, minimally altered the facade. However, in recent years, the imposing design has been altered beyond recognition.

Carrère and Hastings designed another five-story Italianate palazzo for Black, Starr & Frost. The jewelry store moved from Thirty-ninth Street and Fifth Avenue to the southwest corner of Forty-eighth Street in 1912 (fig.22-3). In 1928, the firm merged with Gorham and became known as Black, Starr, Frost & Gorham. In 1932, the Frost name was dropped. Today, the palazzo is unrecognizable behind black "portholes."

In 1907, the Fifth Avenue Presbyterian Church replaced its parsonage with a commercial building that looked like an elegant, but altered residence. The five-story limestone building, at 712 Fifth Avenue, north of Fifty-fifth Street, was designed by Albert Gottleib in the neo-French Classic style. The rusticated ground floor contained an arched entranceway and a shopfront occupying most of the frontage. Above this rested three arched windows with balustrades at the bases and a frieze and dentilled cornice above. The third and fourth floors, designed as a unit, were separated by double-height pilasters with Corinthian capitals. They supported a modillioned cornice beneath a balustrade in front of the fifth floor. The slate mansard story was pierced by three segmentally arched dormers.

The major tenant was L. Alavoine and Company, an interior decorating firm, which remained until the 1950s. The jewelry firm of Cartier occupied the third floor until 1917, when the firm moved to 651 Fifth Avenue. The first floor was initially occupied by art galleries. In 1964, the building held the Rizzoli Bookstore, which remained until 1985.

In 1908, real estate investor Charles Gould hired Woodruff Leeming to design a small commercial building on the site of the adjacent town house. When François Coty leased the marble building in 1910, he commissioned L. Alavoine and Co. to design the interior and René Lalique to design decorative windows for the third through fifth floors. The side windows are etched with intertwining vines and poppies extending up the three floors. The windows, in frosted relief, were originally highlighted with amber. The interior was decorated with Lalique glass as well. Coty remained until 1941; more recent tenants have been unimpressive. The building deteriorated, but the windows, hidden and possibly protected by grime, survived.

It and the adjoining building (known as "Coty/Rizzoli") were designated New York City landmarks in 1985. After meticulous renovation and restoration, the facades have been incorporated (along with the reconstructed 716 Fifth Avenue) into a wonderful design for Henri Bendel's new store (fig. 22-4). For the first time in years, the Lalique windows are gleaming, now an integral part of the Bendel store. Set back fifty feet from the street, the office tower which uses the development rights from the landmarks forms a tall backdrop to these exquisite buildings.

W. & J. Sloane

In 1901, the Windsor Arcade was erected on the site of the Windsor Hotel (fig. 23-1). The three-story building, with a monumental entrance surmounted by freestanding sculpture, was the avenue's—if not the city's—most glorious taxpayer-type structure. Filled with art galleries and smart shops, it was suited to the fairly quiet expanse of the upper Forties.

Just a few years after B. Altman's audacious move, the Windsor Arcade's obituary was written in 1909. W & J. Sloane signed a long-term lease for the northern half of the structure, set to begin at the expiration of the arcade's existing leases.

W. & J. Sloane was the first major store to move that far north. Since the site was across Forty-seventh Street from Miss Helen Gould's home, everyone assumed that she would leave and lease her residence to trade. Whereas the Windsor Hotel had been a meeting place for her father and the Windsor Arcade was a low-scale, genteel place of business, living across the street from a large furniture store was a different matter. A writer mused that ". . . Miss Gould has held the fort in the face of the steady advance of trade up Fifth Avenue to and beyond Forty-seventh Street . . . "[18] She continued to do so. She remained in her brownstone, surrounded by trade, until her death in 1938.

The architectural firm of J. B. Snook's Sons designed the eight-story building for Sloane's retail and wholesale showrooms (fig. 23-2). A row of monumental engaged Ionic columns wrapped around the Indiana limestone facade.

W. & J. Sloane had relocated from Broadway and Ninteenth Street, its home since 1882. (Sloane's also bought 557-561 West 29th Street for a warehouse and workrooms and 541–547 West Twenty-ninth Street for a combination garage and stable.)

The store opened in April, 1912, with its main entrance on Fifth Avenue and a carriage entrance on Forty-seventh Street. Many of its rooms were reproductions of portions of period rooms with all work designed and produced by Sloane employees. The carriage reception room was modeled on an English room designed by Sir Christopher Wren. The second-floor foyer in front of the elevators had walls copied from the drawing room of an English manor home and a ceiling made from plaster impressions of the ceiling of a seventeenth-century English inn. The third floor featured a Louis XVI salon, based on an apartment in the Petit Trianon. W. & J. Sloane did many large-scale furnishing and decorating jobs, including the Biltmore Hotel and various movie palaces. In 1934, the store installed its long-standing "House of Years," a completely furnished home. One woman remembers walking through the house as a newlywed. "It wasn't the usual series of unconnected model rooms, it was a substantial house, and I wanted it all."

The southern half of the Windsor Arcade lasted a few years longer, since its leases were not due to expire until 1911. Robert Goelet leased this portion, which extended to Madison Avenue's new and glamorous Ritz-Carlton Hotel. Architect Charles I. Berg, who had designed the

Fig. 23-1 View north from Forty-sixth Street, ca. 1905. Architect Charles I. Berg's Windsor Arcade, one of New York City's most magnificent temporary structures, has been constructed on the former site of the Windsor Hotel. Helen Gould's home is just across East Forty-seventh Street. The St. Regis Hotel in the distance is across the avenue from the Gotham Hotel, which is under construction. Courtesy: Pace University Archives

arcade, altered this portion into offices.

It was replaced by the 1921 S. W. Strauss banking building designed by Warren and Wetmore. Seymour Durst remembers that the grand building with monumental engaged columns became occupied by the offices of New York's major real estate "operators" by the late 1930s. It later held the offices of the WNEW radio station.

Charles Scribner's Sons

In 1913, the new building for Charles Scribner's Sons replaced Governor Roswell P. Flower's home (fig. 24-1). The building, at 597 Fifth Avenue, was designed by Ernest Flagg, a brother-in-law to Charles Scribner. Years before, Flagg had informally advised his cousin, Alice Gwynne and her husband Cornelius Vanderbilt II, about some room rearrangement in the chateau.

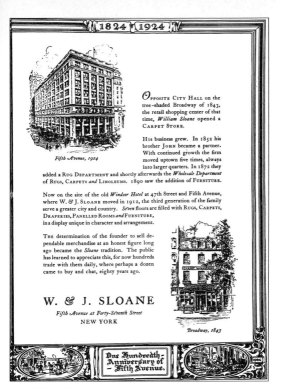

Fig. 23-2 W. & J. Sloane, the grand furniture store, was built on the site of the Windsor Arcade. It was occupied in its last years by E. J. Korvette. Courtesy: Fifth Avenue Association

Impressed, Vanderbilt paid for his education at the École des Beaux-Arts in Paris. It may have been there that Flagg also learned methods of ancient construction. Charles Scribner Jr. remembers that an electrical contractor was hired to modernize the store's lighting. He estimated that the new wiring would take a day to install. "But my great-uncle had used pebbles between the floors and the poor contractor broke every drill bit he had. We showed him mercy and let him leave after he had made one hole—a day's work."

Flagg designed the earlier Scribner building at 155 Fifth Avenue (only recently, but sadly, altered). He also designed the

building at 311 West Forty-third Street, the headquarters of the Scribner Press, where their books were printed and bound.

This eleven-story office building is a designated New York City landmark. But it is also a landmark to generations of readers who entered and knew that either they would find whichever book they desired, or that they would be assisted, in hushed tones and to the greatest extent possible.

The limestone-faced building, although elegant and judiciously ornamented, was subservient to the storefront. The storefront—an elliptical arch of ironwork and glass—looked like a graceful touch of Paris. The double-height expanse of glass, thirteen panes wide and framed by black ironwork columns highlighted in gold, remains so glorious that merchandise is superfluous. And this beauty was practical—the sunlight streamed in and, during the summers, the windows opened. "In the summer, when the sunlight came through the blue and white awnings, being in the store was like being on a beautiful yacht," recalls Mr. Scribner. "This building has given me more joy than I can possibly say."

Upon entering the main salesroom, the visitor is usually struck by its incredible grandeur (fig. 24-2). Soaring thirty feet to a vaulted ceiling, the basilica-like space combines the form of a church, the ambiance of a turn-of-the-century library, and the service of a Fifth Avenue shop. Originally the wide center aisle extended

from the entrance to the grand staircase leading to the mezzanine. Set behind ornamental railings, it was dominated by a huge bookcase. A few stairs on either side led to the balconies, which edged the room with curvilinear cast-iron railings set into piers. They could be reached from the main floor by spiral staircases. "The spiral staircases were lovely," said Mr. Scribner. "But [they were] so difficult for the salespeople to use that we decided to remove one. And the salespeople went on strike because they thought it was too beautiful to destroy. I was so touched."

Changes have occurred over the years, including the installation of new lighting fixtures and movable bookcases which block the central aisle. But the space remains as inspiring as ever.

The building was owned by the Scribner family until 1984. Brentano's, another bookstore formerly located a block to the south, is now housed within the building. Since the landmarked exterior is essentially inviolate, the putti still grip the black sign with gold lettering proclaiming, "Charles Scribner's Sons."

The Triumph of Trade

The Vanderbilt Colony was cushioned on the east side by St. Patrick's Cathedral and on the west side by Columbia University's prohibition against commercial uses on its property between Forty-seventh and Fifty-first streets. The university relaxed its rule

Fig. 24-2 Early view of Charles Scribner's Sons interior. The basilica-like space originally had a wide center aisle extending from the entrance to a vista—in this case, the grand staircase leading to the mezzanine. A few stairs on either side of the mezzanine lead to the balconies, which could be reached from the main floor by spiral staircases; except for the removal of the one on the left the interior has changed little. Courtesy: Charles Scribner, III

Opposite
Fig. 24-1 View of Charles Scribner's Sons Building, ca. 1940s. The grand building was owned by the Scribner family until 1984; it is now occupied by Brentano's. Since the landmarked exterior is essentially inviolate, putti grip the black sign over the storefront that still proclaims, "Charles Scribner's Sons." The Scribner Building is adjacent to a narrow, ivory-colored marble building designed by Severance & Schumm for a china shop. The building at the Forty-ninth Street corner was occupied by McCutcheon. Courtesy: Charles Scribner, III

after it moved to Morningside Heights. Requiring funds, it sold and mortgaged portions of this "upper estate" through the years. In 1904, the university trustees sold the lots between Forty-seventh and Forty-eighty streets, giving preference to leaseholders. Many renters bought their houses on side streets, but only Charles F. Cook, the head of Tiffany & Co., purchased his house on Fifth Avenue.

In March 1907, the university announced that commercial uses would be permitted on the avenue frontage, between Forty-eighth and Fifty-first streets. The *New York Times* commented, "those who like to make excursions into the future are asking how long it will be before [the Vanderbilt houses] will follow the Stewart mansion and other historic residences to the yards of the dealers in second-hand material."[19]

With the restrictions lifted, that portion of the avenue became commercial. The block front between Fiftieth and Fifty-first streets had at one time been occupied by Benjamin Altman, Darius Ogden Mills, Samuel D. Babcock, a banker and president of the New York Chamber of Commerce, and Mrs. Russell Sage. Within a few years of Babcock's 1902 death, a twelve-story apartment house was erected on the site of his house. It was converted to offices. The following year, the builders purchased the adjacent Mills home and replaced it with an eight-story loft. Mr. Altman's home was the last to go. Within two years of his 1913 death, his home was converted for business

and his art gallery replaced by an eight-story loft. By 1915, the entire block front was commercial.

In 1914, Bergdorf Goodman moved to 616 Fifth Avenue, between West Forty-ninth and Fiftieth streets. Edwin Goodman had brought "Goodman's Store" from Lockport, New York, to New York City. He joined forces with a furrier named Herman Bergdorf and within a few years, Goodman bought him out. And the custom specialty shop was his. After a few years at this Fifth Avenue address, he was doing three million dollars' worth of annual business in furs and custom-made suits.

The Stalwart Vanderbilt Colony

Wealthy families attempted their abortive battle against trade as merchants pushed northward from Thirty-fourth and Forty-second streets and southward from Fifty-ninth Street. Within a few years and despite this continuing onslaught, the Cathedral Section or the Vanderbilt Colony remained residential. But the millionaires' haven of a few years before was now constantly under siege.

The Vanderbilts were not content to rely on serendipitous barriers to protect them from trade. Across the avenue from the Twin Houses was the Roman Catholic Orphan Asylum, a handsome neighbor with a large front lawn. The church sold the property in 1900 after the orphanage

moved to the Bronx. Parcels on the quiet side streets were quickly purchased for residential development, whereas the Fifth Avenue frontage sold slowly. The East Fifty-first Street corner was purchased by the Union Club, which held an architectural competition won by Cass Gilbert and John DuFais. The 1902 limestone palazzo had a slightly raised first floor, which permitted lounging members a good view of the avenue (fig. 26-1).

Between 1902–1905, George Washington Vanderbilt, who lived across the street in one of the Twin Houses, erected two homes located between the Union Club and the Morton Plant house. The so-called Marble Twins at 645–647 Fifth Avenue were designed by the recently established architectural firm of Hunt and Hunt, which was headed by the sons of Richard Morris Hunt, who had designed Biltmore, Vanderbilt's North Carolina estate.

The French Beaux-Arts town houses were constructed so that they could be easily joined together. The facades were visually connected by the monumental fluted pilasters with composite capitals above the rusticated base.

The Marble Twins remained in the family for a while. George's sister Emily and her husband William D. Sloane purchased 645 Fifth Avenue for their daughter Lila. She and her husband, William B. Osgood Field, remained there for twenty years, thereby becoming among the last residents to leave the avenue.

The other Twin, 647 Fifth Avenue

had a shorter residential life, but it's the only Vanderbilt mansion that stands today. Robert Goelet and his wife, Elsie Whelan, a Vanderbilt relative, moved in after their 1904 marriage. Their short marriage ended in divorce and he moved. In 1917, the building was acquired by the art dealers Wildenstein & Co., who added one story to the facade, but kept the general configuration of the design fairly intact. They remained until the 1930s when they moved to a new building on the upper east side. The large round arched windows of the main floor were subsequently altered.

Next, George Vanderbilt hired Hunt & Hunt to remodel his city home—the southern Twin House. For two years, it had been occupied by servants. Vanderbilt left the home after the city had forced him to demolish his partially built two-story porte cochere.

Vanderbilt's tenant, Henry Clay Frick of Pittsburgh, was rumored to pay an annual rental in "the six figures." People wondered what his motives were "in becoming a citizen of New York, although it has been said that he has a desire to go into National politics."[20]

Mrs. Frederick Gallatin's home, at the southwest corner of Fifty-third Street adjacent to William K. Vanderbilt Jr.'s home, was the first domino to fall in the Vanderbilt Colony. She leased it to the Brewster Carriage Company in 1909. The newspapers announced ominously, "Trade obtained a new grip on the once impregnable residential section of Fifth Avenue . . . It is the opinion of real estate operators that it is only a matter of time when Fifth Avenue, south of Central Park, will be given over entirely to business."[21] In 1913, jeweler Michael Dreicer leveled the site. He commissioned architect Henry Otis Chapman to design two six-story limestone buildings with Gothic ornament, and the exclusive furriers Revillon Frères moved in. Dreicer was careful to ensure that the structure would be as sympathetic to the Vanderbilt mansion and St. Thomas Church as possible. Aymar Embury II admitted that they showed "a commendable deference to architectural order almost without precedent in New York."[22]

The small Langham Hotel at Fifty-second Street (on property once owned by Madame Restell) was sold to be replaced by an apartment house. Then, W. K. Vanderbilt and W. D. Sloane stepped in. They purchased the property for approximately $1,350,000 and restricted business uses on it. After several transfers, the property was sold to Edward H. Harriman, who died before building a home. In 1909, Harriman's widow and the Vanderbilt interests agreed to lift the restrictions, "furnishing another illustration of the many in select residential parts of the city that an advancing business movement can not be successfully combated for any

Fig. 26-1 View north from Forty-eighth Street showing east side of the avenue, ca. 1905. Visible are the corner of the Buckingham Hotel, St. Patrick's Cathedral, and the recently constructed Union Club, Marble Twins, and the Morton Plant residence. Courtesy: Private Collection

27-1

length of time."[23] Shortly thereafter, the sons of Henry Phipps (Andrew Carnegie's former partner) erected an eight-story loft building (661-663) which was occupied by Hickson's, a women's clothing shop. Subsequently, the building was occupied by Georg Jensen and Sulka, among others.

All of these were small incursions, compared to Levi Morton's 1911 sale of his house. Having occupied the house for eighteen years with Cornelius Vanderbilt and the Criterion Club as his immediate neighbors, he moved to a twenty-four-room apartment on Eighty-first Street and Fifth Avenue. When he sold 681 Fifth Avenue, the *New York Times* headline screamed, "Vanderbilt Colony Invaded by Trade."

Previous page
Fig. 27-1 View across Fifth Avenue of Cartier, formerly the Morton Plant mansion. Architect William Welles Bosworth minimally altered the exterior: He replaced the round-headed openings with square ones and placed the main entrance on the avenue. In 1916, Plant sold the mansion to William K. Vanderbilt, who leased it to Cartier for $50,000 a year. To the right is the Wildenstein & Co. gallery occupying the former "Marble Twin." Courtesy: Cartier

Fig. 27-2 View of Fifty-second Street facade, shortly after building alteration. This facade was originally the main facade, with the round arched central entrance set into the rusticated base. The entrance was emphasized by the central bay composed of a pediment at the fourth floor supported by four fluted Scamozzi Ionic pilasters above a balcony. The fifth-floor windows are part of the design of the frieze and alternate with rinceaux. The Cartier clock on a bollard has since been moved to the Fifth Avenue facade. Across Fifth Avenue is the northern Twin House. Courtesy: Cartier

Morton commissioned McKim, Mead & White to design the new building (extant, lower-floor alterations). The site was leased for a long term to E. P. Dutton & Co., which moved its bookstore from Twenty-third Street where it had been for thirty years. Fortunoff's is currently in the building.

In 1912, the Whitney mansion across from Mrs. Alice Gwynne Vanderbilt's chateau was demolished. In its place on the southwest corner of Fifty-seventh Street, August Heckscher erected a temporary two-story taxpayer.

In 1916, Mrs. W. Seward Webb sold her home at 680 Fifth Avenue adjacent to St. Thomas Church to John D. Rockefeller Jr. He hired William Welles Bosworth to design a six-story commercial building.

The Morton Plant Mansion: New Home to Cartier

The East Fifty-second Street frontage was finally sold, and then resold for the construction of an apartment hotel. With foundation excavations completed, the New York Realty Corporation purchased it on behalf of the Vanderbilt interests to prohibit construction of anything but a single-family residence. In 1903, the East Fifty-second Street property (651 Fifth Avenue) was finally sold to Morton F. Plant. He was vice-president of the Plant Investment Corporation, owned the Eastern (Baseball)

League's New London team, and was a part owner of Philadelphia's National League team. Of his many charitable donations, his $1 million gift to the Connecticut College for Women is most memorable. His residence, completed in 1905, was designed by architect Robert W. Gibson. The six-story town house, in the neo-Italian Renaissance style, epitomized luxurious elegance.

By 1916, with Hickson across the street, the area had become too commercial for Plant. He requested that the trade restriction be removed from his property; instead, W. K. Vanderbilt repurchased the property for one million dollars, abrogated the restrictive covenant and rented it to the Cartier firm for $50,000 a year, the highest rent paid per square foot on the avenue. Plant and his wife moved to a new mansion farther up the avenue, and he died shortly thereafter.

Plant's former home was delicately altered by William Welles Bosworth for Cartier (figs. 27-1, 27-2). The conversion retained the best of the mansion to create a precious setting for jewels. The entrance was moved to Fifth Avenue; its now-famous clock was atop a bollard at the corner. The clock has since been moved to the Fifth Avenue facade. The alteration was well received and the display windows, although described as being "decidedly French" on "the classic and rather Italian palace-type of old house," were considered very close to perfect: "The windows proper are very interesting with a frame of bronze and verde antique marble. The plate glass, which is certainly the most practical material for a shop window, is divided in such an unusual way that the commerciality of the material is entirely lost while the delicate scale and choice materials form a setting for a display of jewelry or bibelots which it would be hard to surpass."[24]

The alteration was discreet and must have been an extremely gentle and genteel neighbor to the remaining nearby mansions. The building was kept largely intact and it later expanded into the adjacent mansion on East Fifty-second Street.

With its intimate spaces and sumptuous finishes, the shop offers a sense of hushed exclusivity (fig. 27-3). In fact, Cartier may be one of the few remaining stores which offers the cosseted luxuriousness that Upper Fifth Avenue once provided to a select few. In 1917, the building was awarded the Fifth Avenue Association's gold medal for an altered building.

St. Thomas Church

Upjohn's St. Thomas Church was destroyed by fire on August 8, 1905. At the time, the cause was thought to be poorly insulated electric wiring which supplied power to the organ. The four-alarm fire brought crowds of men and equipment to the scene, but the water supply was insufficient.

The church was left in ruins, and the adjoining Webb and Twombly homes were severely damaged by water. Works of art were destroyed, including two masterpieces by John LaFarge and Augustus Saint-Gaudens.

Scaffolding was erected around the tower, because the congregation contemplated rebuilding the church. In the end, they decided to donate the tower to a suburban church and erected a temporary wooden structure with seats for twelve hundred (fig. 28-1). The structure, simple by their standards, but quite elaborate by modern ones, was carefully decorated for all holidays. Services were held on the site as the new church was being built around it. As portions of the church were completed, the congregation was able to move out of the temporary structure, which was dismantled, into the actual building. The congregation, however, spent quite a few years in the temporary building. It had generously donated the money it had collected for the reconstruction to assist San Francisco's earthquake victims.

The church held an architectural competition and approved the designs of Cram, Goodhue and Ferguson (fig. 28-2). Their design, of white Kentucky limestone, was unlike any in the city. It reinterpreted French Gothic architecture, with a bit of English Gothic decoration as well.

The cornerstone was laid in 1911 and the first service was held on October 4, 1913. Funerals of famous people included: Joseph Pulitzer (1911), John Jacob Astor (1912), Chauncey Depew (1928), and Brigadier General Cornelius Vanderbilt (1942).

Fig. 27-3 An early view of the shop's interior. Courtesy: Cartier

The New York City Landmarks Preservation Commission designation report admits, "To many, this church is the most beautiful in the City." Whereas St. Patrick's Cathedral was spread over an entire city block and was built when the area was still countrified, St. Thomas Church, at the center of West Fifty-third Street, was in an increasingly urban neighborhood. So, the building's single drawback is that it's difficult to stand far enough away to appreciate it. The asymmetrical facade is dominated by its bold fifteen-story bell tower at the corner and yet balanced by the deeply recessed entrance portal.

Part of the building's beauty may result from its absolute adherence to its period. The building is masonry without a bit of modern steel. Everything from the door hinges to the floor tiles was custom

made for the church. Unlike so many neo-Gothic churches that are all tracery and light, this edifice skillfully joins flat planar lines with delicately carved surfaces. Whereas the feelings of cold exaltation emanate from many Gothic churches, St. Thomas is permeated with tremendous warmth and humanity, as well. It invites one to partake of its beauty.

Over its famous Brides Door, a craftsman carved a dollar sign in place of a lover's knot. Once discovered, the church allowed it to remain, a source of never-ending pleasure for observant pedestrians. Seventy-five years ago, a writer, describing New York's smartest bridal church, said, "On some days in June the beadle runs off fashionable weddings end to end, and all afternoon crowds of eager, excited women wait on the pavement for a glimpse of that composed little face in a filmy cloud of white which is the latest bride."[25]

Guests on the Avenue

As commercial palaces were being constructed south of Forty-second Street, "skyscraper" hotels were built at the upper end of the avenue, bracketing the residents. The city's most luxurious hotels, many of which had originated in the nineteenth century, formed the terminus of the commercial avenue and framed the entrance to Central Park.

When new, they looked like a version of Stonehenge towering over low

mansions. With sumptuous appointments and superb service, these hotels offered the city's best to its wealthiest visitors. Not as large as the dark, brownstone Waldorf-Astoria, these modern marble buildings offered far more exclusivity.

The St. Regis Hotel

The 1901-1904 St. Regis Hotel has always been one of the city's most elegant Beaux-Arts style buildings, from its lustrous brass and copper kiosk to its high mansard roof (figs. 29-1, 29-2). It was built for Colonel John Jacob Astor IV on a site he and his mother had earlier considered before building their new home on Fifth Avenue and East Sixty-fifth Street.

Named after Lake St. Regis in the Adirondacks, Trowbridge and Livingston's opulent hotel was the area's tallest structure (fig. 29-3). In 1927, the firm of Sloan and Robertson designed a limestone extension on East Fifty-fifth Street which doubled the hotel's size. The design is far more simple and subdued than the original and forms a tasteful backdrop to this beauty.

With every inch of the small public rooms covered with sumptuous materials, the St. Regis Hotel's self-contained world of luxury was far more selective than the massive Waldorf-Astoria's. This hotel had a quiet, almost clublike atmosphere.

Opposite

Fig. 29-2 This view is of the St. Regis Hotel's mansard roof after its recent restoration. A bracketed cornice supports the mansard roof, which is pierced by dormers. Courtesy: St. Regis Hotel

Fig. 29-3 View looking south from West Fifty-sixth Street at the east side of the avenue, ca. 1904. The brand new St. Regis Hotel towers above the Colford-Jones row of houses across East Fifty-fifth Street. From this photo, it is evident that the St. Regis Hotel was designed in three sections, like a classical column: base, shaft, and capital. Courtesy: St. Regis Hotel

Fig. 29-4 This early view shows an opulent marble-lined hall in the hotel. Courtesy: St. Regis Hotel

Exclusivity must have been very important to the son of the woman who started "The Four Hundred." Colonel Astor died in the *Titanic* disaster of 1912 and his son, Vincent Astor, took over.

Colonel Astor's wife designed the interiors, including the exotic Salle Cathay. Each room had a thermostat to allow guests to select heated, moistened, dried, or cooled air. A central vacuum cleaning system allowed maids to attach a tube to an outlet in each room and have the dust sucked down to the basement. Stairways and corridors were lined with marble (figs. 29-4, 29-5). Furniture for the public rooms was purchased in Europe; Arnold Constable provided the bedroom and suite furniture (fig. 29-6). China was Royal Worcester,

Fig. 29-5 This early view shows one of the dining rooms in the St. Regis Hotel. Courtesy: St. Regis Hotel

Minton, and two sets of Royal Sèvres. Scattered throughout were forty-seven Steinway pianos; the hotel featured a three thousand-book library.

This exquisite building, however, was not enthusiastically welcomed by its neighbors. But attempts to stop trade, no matter how divine the impetus, were at best temporary. In 1904 and 1905, the recently opened hotel suffered through two attempts to have its state liquor license repealed. The Fifth Avenue Presbyterian Church congregation alleged that the hotel violated the excise law because its entrance was within two hundred feet of the church. In response, the hotel changed a Fifth Avenue entrance into a window; its main entrance remained on Fifty-fifth Street. After that

Fig. 29-6 This early view shows a typical suite in the St. Regis Hotel with furnishings supplied by Arnold Constable & Co. Courtesy: St. Regis Hotel

strategy failed, some neighbors claimed that the hotel manager had made errors in his license application. By undercounting the number of dwellings within a specified radius of the hotel entrance, they alleged that the eight consents received from property owners were less than the required two-thirds. The commissioner of excise refused the congregation's request.

During the appeal, the manager was reported as saying, "I cannot understand what the motive of these persons may be. We make a specialty of being quiet; surely a house like this could not be run as a noisy place. As to the carriages, which I have heard complained of—why we have no very large banquet hall, and there are never more than one or two carriages at the door. The only way that I can explain this move is that they want us to buy up the property around here . . ."[26]

Actually, he was completely wrong. William Rockefeller, the occupant of 689 Fifth Avenue, purchased numbers 3, 5, and 7 East Fifty-fourth Street to ensure that the hotel would not open a trade entrance on "his" street.

The Gotham Hotel

A year after the St. Regis Hotel opened, the Gotham Hotel opened across Fifth Avenue on a portion of the former St. Luke's property (figs. 29-7, 29-8). Designed by Hiss and Weeks, this handsome limestone building forms the other half of the monumental gateway to the splendors of what was then referred to as "Upper Fifth Avenue."

A few months later, the church tried to prevent the as-yet-unoccupied Gotham Hotel (now the Peninsula Hotel) from obtaining a license. Across West Fifty-fifth Street, the hotel would have been very hard pressed to prove it was farther than two hundred feet away. However, a bill was rushed through the legislature to amend the Raines law and, "for the protection of respectable hotels," in effect allow hotels with at least two hundred guest rooms above the basement to be close to churches.

The University Club

The other portion of the hospital property was purchased by the University Club, ready to move uptown from Madison Square. (The Union Club had originally been interested in the parcel, but the deal fell through.). In 1900, McKim, Mead & White designed a granite palazzo as the clubhouse. The nine-story building— looking like a very tall three stories—was decorated with shields of American universities. The designated New York City landmark remains, many shades darker than it was when it opened. Reading newspapers by the windows, old men look as if they had been sitting there since college graduation.

The Plaza Hotel

Meanwhile, Henry Hardenburgh, the architect of the Waldorf-Astoria, was hired to design the Plaza Hotel to replace an earlier one which was more like the old Savoy and Netherland hotels than the newer hotels (figs. 29-9, 29-10). The developer announced that the exclusive and absolutely first-class hotel would resemble London's Carlton House. Although portions of the domed interior did resemble it, the hotel was fairly French. The white limestone and terra-cotta skyscraper was capped by a green mansard roof accentuated by dormers and cresting. With its perfect park-side location and glorious public rooms and private suites, the Plaza became an immediate favorite with wealthy and noble guests. All of these new hotels of white marble made the Waldorf-Astoria look passé the way the marble mansions had made the brownstone homes look dated.

In 1905, the Hotel Savoy at Fifty-ninth Street announced the construction of an eleven-story annex and that the Hotel Bolkenhayn would be run as well as an annex.

Grand Army Plaza, the large open square in front of the entrance to Central Park, was marked by two additions. An equestrian statue of William Tecumseh Sherman, designed by Augustus Saint-Gaudens, was erected in 1903 at the park entrance. In the center of the plaza, the Pulitzer Memorial Fountain was constructed in 1915. Above the basins, a bronze female figure of Abundance carried a basket of fruits of the earth. Both of these monuments had fallen into disrepair and have been restored. The limestone fountain, designed by Carrère and Hastings, was so deteriorated that it was practically rebuilt in sturdier granite. The regilded Sherman statue, however, was criticized by some for its startling brightness. Freestanding columns and balustrades which were part of the original plan for the plaza were removed in the 1930s and have not yet been replaced.[27]

Chain Stores

Little construction occurred during and after World War I, but there was much movement onto and off of the avenue. Two moves to Fifth Avenue were about as unrelated to Vanderbilts, custom-made

29-7

29-8

clothing, or fancy florists as possible. They were chain operations—Child's and Woolworth's.

In 1917, the F. W. Woolworth Company leased the northeast corner of Fortieth Street, in the center of the shopping district. Reports that the company had been looking for a Fifth Avenue address had been dismissed as a joke. The property was leased for forty-two years at an aggregate rental of $4.5 million.

Five-story buildings and old brownstones altered for commercial use were demolished for the Woolworth's building designed by Jardine, Hill & Murdock. The upper floors were leased for office space and the ground floor and basement were to be used as Woolworth's salesroom. H. T. Parson, vice-president and treasurer, responded to the shocked critics about the store's presence on the avenue. "There seems to be an impression that we are 'invading' Fifth Avenue. We do not consider that we are doing any such thing. We are simply following the trend of business . . . the very shops that will now be neighbors to us were our neighbors in the old days when Sixth Avenue was the fashionable shopping district. . . . We see nothing strange in entering Fifth Avenue. The name means nothing to us. We are simply going where the business is and if business had centered itself in Fourth Avenue, instead of Fifth, it would be Fourth Avenue to which we would now move."[28]

In 1919, at 377 Fifth Avenue, between Thirty-fifth and Thirty-sixth streets, the Norrie family sold their former home on property they had owned since 1856 to the Childs Corporation. "The invasion by a Childs 'beanery' in that aristocratic section of the avenue, close to Tiffany's and Altman's aroused considerable excitement among the merchants and certain members of the Fifth Avenue Association. Architecturally, the new building is as satisfactory as most of the other small . . . loft structures, and since Woolworth's 5-and-10 cent stores holds forth with every evidence of popular patronage a few blocks to the north there is nothing strange in the location of a Childs eating house close to Tiffany's."[29]

So within fifteen years of B. Altman's audacious move, Woolworth's and Child's quietly moved onto the Avenue. Although there was no applause, it was accepted as progress.

Previous page
Fig. 29-7 View from East Fifty-fifth Street to the Gotham Hotel prior to its renovation and rebirth as the Peninsula Hotel. Photo: Carl Forster. Courtesy: New York City Landmarks Preservation Commission

Fig. 29-8 This contemporary view shows the lobby entrance of the Peninsula Hotel reincarnated in the art nouveau style.
Courtesy: Peninsula Hotel

Opposite
Fig. 29-9 Contemporary view of the Plaza Hotel across Fifth Avenue from Sixtieth Street. Augustus Saint-Gaudens's statue of General William Tecumseh Sherman following the Angel of Victory is in the foreground. The 1907 Plaza Hotel, a loose adaptation of the French Reniassance style, was built on the site of an old-fashioned hotel, also called the Plaza.
Courtesy: Plaza Hotel

Fig. 29-10 Contemporary view of the Plaza Hotel's Edwardian Room, overlooking Central Park. It is one of the many dining and public spaces in the hotel that evoke early twentieth-century opulence. Courtesy: Plaza Hotel

1. *Real Estate Record and Guide*, April 20, 1901, p. 694.

2. *New York Times*, December 31, 1911.

3. *New York Times*, May 3, 1911.

4. Fifth Avenue Association, *Fifty Years on Fifth*, pp, 40, 46.

5. A. C. David, "The New Fifth Avenue," *Architectural Record*, July 1907, p. 2.

6. Alfred H. Taylor, "Reconstructed Business House Fronts in New York," *Architectural Record*, July, 1907, p. 13.

7. *New York Times*, October 5, 1934.

8. A. C. David, "The New Fifth Avenue," *Architectural Record*, July 1907, p. 11.

9. *Real Estate Record and Guide*, December 17, 1904, p. 1346.

10. *New York Times*, October 16, 1910.

11. Christopher Gray, "A Delicate Work of Ceramic in the Path of a Tower," *New York Times*, July 22, 1990.

12. *New York Times*, May 27, 1909.

13. *New York Times*, January 29, 1911.

14. *New York Times*, June 27, 1909.

15. *New York Times*, August 13, 1911.

16. *New York Times*, June 2, 1903.

17. C. Matlack Price, "A Renaissance in Commercial Architecture," *Architectural Record*, May 1912, pp. 453-454.

18. *New York Times*, November 5, 1909.

19. *New York Times*, March 5, 1907.

20. *New York Times*, November 27, 1909.

21. Ibid.

22. Aymar Embury II, "From Twenty-third Street Up," *The Brickbuilder*, November 1916, p. 286.

23. *New York Times*, September 3, 1911.

24. William Lawrence Bottemley, "The Architecture of Retail Stores," *Architectural Forum*, June 1924, p. 236.

25. Will Irwin, *Highlights of Manhattan*, p. 213.

26. *New York Times*, January 12, 1905.

27. Paul Goldberger, "A Restored Grand Army Plaza, With a New Coat for the General," *New York Times*, June 28, 1990.

28. *New York Times*, July 29, 1917.

29. *New York Times*, July 25, 1920.

PART THREE

From Tiffany's to Trump Tower

A Miracle Mile

People who elevated shopping to a religion found over a mile of temples along Fifth Avenue. Every bright bauble from simulated pearls to a diamond tiara was sold on the glittering thoroughfare between B. Altman at Thirty-fourth Street and Bergdorf Goodman at Fifty-eighth Street.

The wares were displayed in buildings illustrating fifty years of fashionable architectural styles. The soft limestone of neo-Gothic spires and Beaux-Arts cartouches vied with the hard-edged stone of art deco towers. The occasional long-converted town house reminded pedestrians of the avenue's residential past. "Fifth Avenue was the one place that money could buy happiness," remembers an elderly shopper. "Fifth Avenue" had become an international symbol for the very best. Everything gleamed—from the smallest fifteen-foot-wide shop to the largest building. Shopkeepers were exceedingly proud of the address. Even the avenue's streetlights were special. The fare for its buses was higher than for other city buses.

But a ride up Fifth Avenue was worth it. The view from the top of a double-decked bus was the most glorious of all. The quintessential New York experience offered a low bird's-eye view of everything as the bus lumbered through traffic. Window shoppers gazed at display windows, fashion critics observed pedestrians' clothing, and architecture lovers looked at the buildings. One of the few opportunities we have now to see that view is to look at the background of Judy Garland's ride up the avenue in *The Clock*.

Strictly speaking, the avenue's peak was short. Even as the exclusive stores continued to offer the world's finest merchandise, here and there a moderately priced shoe store or a dime store elbowed its way onto the grand thoroughfare.

By the 1920s, prewar Fifth Avenue had become a dim memory. During the war, the press had condemned the invasion of trade into the millionaires' village. Previously considered "Upper Fifth Avenue," the thoroughfare had become part of midtown Manhattan in less than a generation. Commuters rushed into the area by bus, subway or train to work in the offices and stores. Residents who remained on the avenue south of Fifty-ninth Street seemed like quaint anachronisms. After all, Fifth Avenue was a street on which to spend money—not to live. "You could spend your buying life on Fifth Avenue," said one wealthy woman who did.

Writers chronicling Fifth Avenue no longer followed the scent of blue bloods. Instead, they sought the opinions of real estate experts. After purchasing an old landmark to demolish it, a developer was asked if he liked the building. He answered, "I would have added $150,000 to the price if [it wasn't] on the land at all."[1]

Of course, most residents had moved north of Fifty-ninth Street at the first or second whiff of trade in the neighborhood. But many of the houses that remained until the 1920s were among the city's finest. These mansions were our ancient castles; they belonged to our aristocracy. So it seemed shocking that these monuments, built to last for ages, were pulverized in such quick succession. These solid "landmarks" were replaced by office buildings or stores, often constructed by or for upstart immigrants. Conspicuous consumption by avenue residents was superseded by lavish consumption by avenue shoppers.

Perfectly located for business, the mansions' taxes and assessments had risen rapidly. It became prohibitively expensive to maintain homes—particularly ones that were infrequently occupied. Even Vanderbilts stopped clinging to their residences in the midst of the tidal wave of trade. And, as the clubs had earlier followed the wealthy to the avenue, now they followed them off the avenue. For instance, the Union, Union League, and Democratic clubs moved north or east.

Many mansions that had been converted to shops still remain. By 1935, only four residences remained on the avenue (they have since been demolished). They continued to serve as the family "town" residences as long as their owners were alive. Two unpretentious brownstones at the corners of East Forty-seventh Street and Forty-eighth Street belonged to Helen Gould Shepard and Robert Goelet, respectively. Helen Gould Shepard died in 1938; her house was closed in 1942 after the death of her husband and torn down in 1952. The Goelet house was demolished in 1942.

The southern "Twin," at the northwest corner of Fifty-first Street, was occupied by Brigadier General Cornelius Vanderbilt, and 645 Fifth Avenue (one of the Marble Twins) was the city residence of W. B. Osgood Field. The Twin mansion was demolished in 1947, and Best & Co.'s 1947 building replaced 645 Fifth Avenue.

In a similar vein, it appears that many remarkable buildings were demolished, while small, innocuous structures survived. It wasn't chance that the Waldorf-Astoria and the Vanderbilt chateaux departed, it was practicality. It was easier, after all, for a real estate developer to purchase a large piece of property under single ownership rather than to deal with several owners to form an assemblage.

After the major wave of construction in the late 1920s and 1930s, a few buildings were constructed in the 1950s and 1960s. But the stores and buildings remained intact for the most part until the 1970s. The avenue's apparent stability was a contrast from the city of transit strikes, school decentralization, and Pennsylvania Station's demolition. And suddenly, the avenue underwent another of its accelerated metamorphoses: Within a few years, DePinna, Best & Co., and The Tailored Woman shut their doors. Sleek glass towers rose in their places.

Triggered by the closings and proliferation of airlines and banks eager for the advertising opportunities of a Fifth Avenue address, the City Planning Commission amended the zoning. The 1972 Fifth Avenue Special District encouraged *real* retail uses on the ground floors with residential units above. This was to ensure retail continuity on the street frontage, and a twenty-four-hour presence by the hotel or apartment residents. Through the years, the zoning has sought to protect the avenue's identity, through signage and street wall requirements, as well.

And, luckily for the avenue's enchanting limestone, the New York City Landmarks Preservation Commission was established in 1965. Designated landmarks, ranging from the New York Public Library to the B. Altman building, are protected from destruction and debasement. One can only wonder how the avenue would have looked if the commission had come into existence earlier. The landmarks that have been incorporated into larger structures like the Knox building, Coty/Rizzoli, or even Saks Fifth Avenue help to maintain the scale and stone texture so important to the avenue while giving property owners the rights to develop way into the sky.

The avenue's ambiance owes a debt of gratitude to the ever-vigilant Fifth Avenue Association as well. It continued to vociferously oppose "boom" (temporary) stores. Since buildings constructed before the 1916 Zoning Resolution had "grandfathered" uses—those that existed prior to the enactment of the zoning—some manufacturing uses had not left the avenue. Through the arts of ostracism and gentle persuasion, the association was able to convince millinery manufacturers to leave the avenue. In 1932 it celebrated Fifth Avenue Week to commemorate its—and the commercial avenue's—twenty fifth-anniversary. All along the avenue, stores, banks, and institutions displayed historic artifacts relating to its history. The association continues to represent the interests of the merchants, while protecting the avenue for shoppers, tourists, and pedestrians. It has become involved with a Business Improvement District, reducing the proliferation of street peddlers and maintaining the quality of the avenue.

Fifth Avenue:
A Shopper's Paradise

Mercantile Fifth Avenue was mobile. Like wealthy New Yorkers climbing up the social ladder, the stores kept pace with demographic changes and the vagaries of fashion.

The avenue was like a banquet table with guests moving around between courses. Best & Co. and Bonwit Teller moved north, Mark Cross and The Tailored Woman moved around, and W. & J. Sloane moved south. Having opened as small specialty shops, stores like Bergdorf Goodman and Peck & Peck grew and moved to larger quarters. Saks arrived on Fifth Avenue. Even Tiffany left its palazzo on East Thirty-seventh Street for a building on East Fifty-seventh Street that looked like a giant vault. Tiffany had coexisted with Woolworth's on the same avenue, but when the neighboring dime stores outnumbered the jewelry stores, it moved farther uptown.

By the 1930s, some shops moved to Madison Avenue or to Fifty-seventh Street; those that remained consolidated on the avenue north of Forty-ninth Street. The avenue's reputation and retail strength was reinforced by this concentration. Safeguarded by Saks and Bergdorf Goodman, small exclusive shops like Kargere, Sulka, Mark Cross, and Cartier clustered with the old posh hotels and deluxe beauty salons. High society paid the high prices for the intensely personal attention and exclusive goods. And, specialty stores had a tremendous amount of out-of-town business in the days before massive suburban malls.

The streetscape south of Forty-second Street had already been transformed in the early years of the century. The department stores ended their northward movement and instead modernized their facilities and expanded to suburban branch stores. B. Altman, Arnold Constable, and Lord & Taylor continued to serve as southern anchors.

During the somber 1930s, the avenue remained the city's foremost shopping street, but took a downturn as many moderately priced stores moved near these department stores. True to their dry goods emporium roots of giving the best quality for the lowest prices, many department stores opened "budget shops" on upper floors to expand their clientele. Not a single department store closed during the Depression; in fact, several were able to purchase their buildings at lowered prices. During this time, a number of very narrow stores, with maximized show windows, opened along the avenue. The 1939 World's Fair brought tourists into New York—and onto Fifth Avenue. Many of the department stores created departments—somewhere between tasteful and tacky—which offered souvenirs like silk scarves of "Landmarks of New York" ($1.00) and silk nightgowns printed with World's Fair logos ($5.95).

As America emerged from the Depression, the stores became glamorous again. After World War II, high spirits returned to the Easter Parade. Approximately 1,250,000 people strolled in the 1947 parade, for instance. For the first time in years, women were seen wearing yards of fabric—dresses with fuller skirts and longer jackets.

The stores continued on, their merchandise trustworthy, their customers reliable. Retailers did much in their power to ensure that women didn't leave these heavenly aisles. They opened restaurants; they extended credit to single working women. The stores made women feel comfortable; during World War I they boosted tremendous sales of Liberty Bonds. Through the years, before cash machines, department stores were among the few places to cash a check when banks were closed.

Until World War II, Paris remained the style mecca. Practically every store had a department which carried good copies of French originals. By 1924, half of all of the clothing manufactured in the United States was made in New York, but there were few famous American fashion designers.

With limited importing of French goods during World War II, stores began to promote American designers. Fashion publicist Eleanor Lambert remembers that Bonwit Teller was one of the few stores to advertise American designer clothes before World War II. Saks, for instance, replaced all labels with their own, because they felt that "the Saks label should be enough."

Through the years, each store

bought exclusive rights for European and American designers. Even into the 1960s, the clothes of various designers like Pucci, Chanel, and B. H. Wragge could only be purchased in a single store. Because they needed to maintain a large pool of customers, the stores retained these designer departments at the same time they carried moderately priced clothing, usually for younger women. Department stores were all things to all shoppers.

In fact, the stores responded to the drastic clothing changes and proliferation of youth-oriented boutiques in the 1960s by creating their own "boutiques." Even the most staid of stores—Arnold Constable—opened Chicatique, not to be confused with DePinella of DePinna, Saks Fifth Avenue's Young Elite, or Lord & Taylor's Discovery Shop.

Fifth Avenue was a shopper's

Fig. 32-1 A group portrait of Saks Fifth Avenue's elevator operators, ca. 1970. In keeping with Adam Gimbel's devotion to personal service, Saks was one of the last of Fifth Avenue's large stores to install escalators. Courtesy: Saks Fifth Avenue

paradise, with the two extremities filled with stores. *Highlights of Manhattan* described traveling up Fifth Avenue in the upper deck of an open-top double-decked bus. After crossing Thirty-fourth Street, the writer felt as if he entered "[the main gate of] the Woman's City, the Ladies' Acre, the eight or ten square blocks . . . which the spending sex holds as its very own."[2] And women were what made the avenue such a grand spectacle. The well-dressed women paraded for each other, for themselves, for their male admirers. Fifth Avenue was a place to be dressed up and be seen.

"My mother always made me wear white gloves on Fifth Avenue," remembers a woman of her shopping excursions in the 1950s. And a 1939 guide for women advised visitors that sports clothes weren't worn in Manhattan by well-dressed New Yorkers. Sleeveless dresses in the daytime were considered "vulgar" and white shoes were *never* worn by well-dressed people.

During this period, the avenue stores were open from 9:00 A.M. to 5:30 P.M., Monday through Saturday, with a few minor variations. During July and August, in those days before air-conditioning, all of the Fifth Avenue department stores closed on Saturdays, and Saturday afternoons in late June and early September. As late as 1937, the Fifth Avenue Association opposed evening shopping hours for retail stores because it believed that the prestige and character of the avenue would be harmed. By the 1960s, many of the stores finally opened late on Thursday nights, but most of them remained closed on Saturdays during summer, long after the installation of air-conditioning.

Unlike Macy's, the Fifth Avenue stores did not rush to acquire escalators. In the late 1930s, B. Altman installed escalators. Until the 1970s, Saks continued to transport their customers on elevators operated by people wearing uniforms and white gloves (fig. 32-1).

Charge accounts became recognized by charge-a-plates, small metal lozenge shapes embossed with the customer's name and account number. Several stores issued a single plate so that a notch in the edge corresponded to a specific store. Lord & Taylor and B. Altman honored each other's plate. The plates evolved into plastic charge cards. But several of the posher stores, including Bergdorf Goodman, Bonwit Teller, and Tiffany, didn't issue them until the 1970s and 1980s . Previously, women merely signed for their purchases.

The twice-yearly sales were major events, particularly before the advent of large numbers of discount stores. They offered the only way for most women to purchase Fifth Avenue merchandise at lower prices. Occasionally, the police had to be called in to close the stores because of the surly crowds. Some stores, like Arnold Constable, were known for particularly good fall anniversary sales.

During this period, many retailers achieved extraordinary success. Unlike modern times with management teams and investment groups, many of these stores reflected the vision of one person: These multimillion-dollar enterprises were run almost as family businesses. Many of the retailers started as poor boys in menial jobs in other department stores and epitomized the Horatio Alger rags-to-riches story. Those who continued in their family businesses expanded them tremendously and ran the stores with a personal touch. Until recently, a Goodman headed Bergdorf Goodman; there were plenty of Pecks in the management of Peck & Peck; Russeks was headed by a Russek; Saks was headed by a Gimbel. These merchants also encouraged extraordinary women to succeed in management, advertising, and design. Their vision, tremendous talent, and diligence helped to propel Dorothy Shaver, Hortense Odlum, Sophie Gimbel, and Sarah Pennoyer, among others, to fame in the world of Fifth Avenue stores.

Display Windows

America was constantly changing, and department stores catered to this desire for change. Staid emporiums patrolled by gentlemen floorwalkers gave way to stores with verve and style. But people needed to be enticed to buy—the new, the novel, the foreign. And display windows became the vehicles. As Lord & Taylor's president Dorothy Shaver stated in 1955, "Look at Fifth Avenue, show window of the apparel industry, the greatest fashion boulevard in the world" (fig. 33-1).

Window shopping, a sport that had begun on the Ladies Mile, had evolved into a fine art. And Fifth Avenue display directors were among the world's best: Henry Callahan, Tom Lee, Gene Moore, Dana O'Clare, Robert Benzio. In 1939 architectural critic Lewis Mumford noted the avenue's "special character of being one long display window."[3] Window displays, ephemeral works of art, were like the excerpts of Broadway shows shown on the "Ed Sullivan Show." Their beauty and style were exciting even if the viewer didn't have the money to shop in the store.

Window shoppers were advised to walk from the west side of Fifth Avenue and Thirty-fourth Street to Forty-sixth Street.

Fig. 33-1 View from East Fifty-third Street looking north, ca. 1938. Arched windows display giftware in the former Cammeyer shoe shop, built on the site of Cornelius Vanderbilt III's home. Dorothy Gray's beauty salon is the second building from the Fifty-fourth Street corner. The building across Fifty-fourth Street with the rounded corners is the Aeolian Building, which contains Elizabeth Arden's beauty salon. Courtesy: Municipal Archives, Department of Records and Information Services, City of New York

Fig. 33-2 This display window from Lord & Taylor, ca. World War I, is a static still life; early wax mannequins melted under the hot lights. Courtesy: Collection of Professor Robert Hoskins

After crossing to the east side, they were to walk to Fifty-eighth Street, turn east to Madison Avenue, and south to Forty-fifth Street (Abercrombie and Fitch) and back to Fifth Avenue.

Secure about their established clientele, specialty stores exhibited one or two perfect examples of their merchandise in an appropriate setting. But department stores, keying the display cards to newspaper advertisements, opened new territory. With windows changed frequently, the designers created a steady stream of dreams for shoppers.

In the early years of the century display windows were static still lifes. Often a clutter of merchandise was placed before real antiques, elaborate textiles or a vase of oversized silk flowers (fig. 33-2). Then, various technological advances allowed display directors great latitude. Just before World War I, lifelike wax mannequins became available—although the hot lights reduced their life spans.

Designer Norman Bel Geddes created abstract mannequins and built a permanent and unornamented background for Franklin Simon's windows in the 1920s (fig. 33-3). In the 1930s mannequins began to look similar to modern ones although they remained fairly static. "Greta Garbo" and "Joan Crawford" models had plaster bodies and stuffed cloth arms. At the same time, Lester Gaba created his "Gaba Girls" modeled after New York socialites (fig. 33-4). Fluorescent lighting was used in display windows after its introduction at the 1939 World's Fair. It reduced wattage and showed the color of merchandise more accurately (fig. 33-5).

Fig. 33-3 Window shoppers study Franklin Simon's display windows, ca. 1930s. The doll-size mannequins model clothing at the time of day it should be worn. Franklin Simon's logo on the glass denotes the year of the shop's establishment on the avenue—1902. Photo: Irving Browning. Courtesy: New-York Historical Society, New York City

Our own Boudoir Greatcoat,
of Kenwood Blanket Cloth
or
Vanity begins at home.

33-4

By the late 1930s, stagy sets were becoming visually boring and they gave way to those with a touch of surrealism. Saks Fifth Avenue commissioned artist Marcel Vertes to design a window. He placed a mannequin on an analyst's couch with her unconscious wish above her—a new Saks dress.[4]

Bonwit Teller's display director in the late 1930s, Tom Lee, designed many surreal windows that to our eyes now seem perfectly chic and modern. Witty and elegant, the windows transcend time and dress styles (figs. 33-6, 33-7, 33-8). The viewer was enticed not merely by the extravagantly expensive clothing and jewels, but also by the three-dimensional environment which was often punctuated with humor. With whimsical touches like dogs made of fabric matching a suit, a moving cloud-filled sky advertising "Heaven Scent," or a hollowed tree trunk holding shelves, Lee's windows, like works of art, required concentration from the viewer. By reducing the window frames to a fairly small size, the displays became intimate spaces which skewed the usual sense of scale.

Several hundred people would gather on Wednesday nights to watch the weekly changing of Bonwit Teller's windows. Lee's wife, Sarah Tomerlin Lee, then an

advertising copywriter for the store, recalls that in 1939 Lee designed possibly the most notorious of all window displays until that time: two "Salvador Dali" windows.

Dali had come into the city the day before and the two men worked all night on them. "Midnight Green" set a male figure posed like Rodin's *The Thinker* behind a

Fig. 33-5 This B. Altman window, ca. 1940, shows the early use of fluorescent lighting. Photo: Worsinger. Courtesy: Collection of Professor Robert Hoskins

female mannequin wrapped in a dark sheet on a bed. "Narcissus White" had a background of pink satin walls studded with mirrors. In the center sat a claw-footed tub covered by Persian lamb and filled with white hands holding hand mirrors. A mannequin with blond waist-length hair, infested with bugs, and scantily dressed in a boa, was just about to step into the tub.

The next morning, Mrs. Lee went to the store. When she saw the windows, which were still curtained from Fifth

Avenue, she advised her husband to make himself scarce. After the windows were unveiled, a group of women complained to the president. Mrs. Odlum then asked for the curtain to be closed. After adding smartly dressed mannequins (one wearing midnight green and the other in narcissus white) and removing some of the more shocking props, the store reopened the windows.

Unaware of the modifications, Dali and his wife brought some friends to see the windows before having a drink in the St. Regis Hotel. Alarmed at what he saw, the artist went into the store and stepped into the window. Inadvertently he pushed the water-filled tub through the window.

From their perch at the top of a double-decked bus, two policemen saw the crowd gathering at the scene. They carried an enraged Dali through the store, yelling "Tom Lee, Tom Lee" before he was locked in the basement storeroom.

Bonwit's sued Dali. That evening, he appeared in night court. Mrs. Lee remembers his friends, extravagantly chic

Opposite
Fig. 33-6 One of Tom Lee's playful windows for Bonwit Teller, ca. 1940, leaves the viewer with a smile. Photo: Worsinger. Courtesy: Collection of Sarah Tomerlin Lee

33-8

33-9

Fig. 33-11 This Lord & Taylor window was designed by Henry Callahan, ca. 1940s. Sophisticated evening wear in black and white is displayed in front of antiques and a painting in grisaille applied directly to the Caen stone. The stolen glance between the gentleman and the woman in white is a characteristic Callahan touch. Courtesy: Collection of Professor Robert Hoskins

Fig. 33-12 Through the years, Lord & Taylor has devoted many windows to public service. This poignant example is from World War II. Collection of Professor Robert Hoskins

Previous pages
Fig. 33-7 Tom Lee's window design for Bonwit Teller, ca. late 1930s, is a witty look at the rustic world. The elegant wood nymph opens her tree trunk filled with accessories, mostly gloves, as naked hands form the ground cover around the base of the tree. Photo: Virginia Roehl. Courtesy: Collection of Sarah Tomerlin Lee

Fig. 33-8 Designed by Tom Lee for Bonwit Teller, this window coordinates with an exhibition of Trompe l'Oeil at the Julien Levy Gallery. Photo: Worsinger. Courtesy: Collection of Sarah Tomerlin Lee

Fig. 33-9 This partially submerged window, designed by Henry Callahan for Lord & Taylor, took advantage of an innovative design: The floors of the display windows sank to the basement to be "trimmed" out of public view. Courtesy: Collection of Professor Robert Hoskins

Opposite
Fig. 33-10 Display designer Henry Callahan works beneath Lord & Taylor's Fifth Avenue windows. Courtesy: Collection of Professor Robert Hoskins

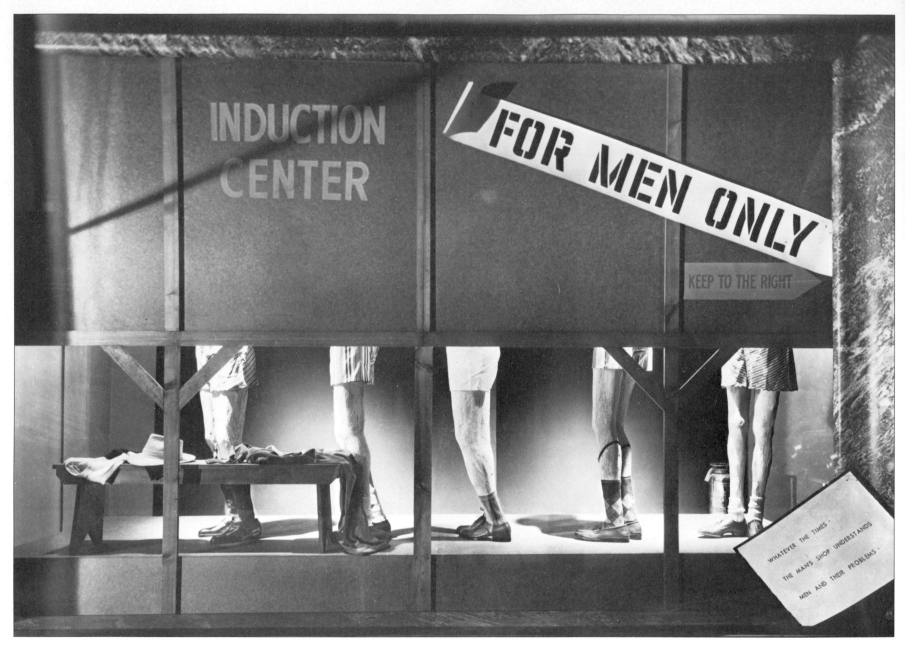

Fig. 33-13 Lord & Taylor's window of "papier maché" legs combines public service with a sales pitch. Courtesy: Lord & Taylor

Schiaparelli employees, sitting in the first two rows in front of prostitutes and alcoholics. Wearing face powder that glowed with a greenish tint, Dali approached the bench. The judge broke out into hysterical laughter and fined him $500.

When Tom Lee returned from his World War II duties as a camouflage expert overseas, he didn't return to Bonwit Teller.

Instead, he designed windows for Bergdorf's, Delman Shoes, and other shops, redecorated many of the departments in Bergdorf, and the interiors of the Plaza and the Savoy-Plaza hotels. He designed costumes and curtains for Broadway and even created floats for Fifth Avenue parades.

Lord & Taylor's show windows, with backgrounds of Caen stone ornamented in

the Adam style, were innovatively designed in 1914. The floors of the windows sank to the basement mezzanine by automatic lift. After they were "trimmed" out of public view (as they are to this day), they were raised back to the street level (fig. 33-9). This was the first and possibly only example of such windows. Each night, a large display window used to rise to occupy the

Fifth Avenue vestibule.

In November 1938, display director Dana O'Clare created "blizzard windows" by frosting the edges of the plate glass with beer and epsom salts and blowing bleached corn flakes around the space. Shoppers listened to the gusting winds. They read the display card that warned, "It's coming— sooner or later." And they purchased winter coats. The Fifth Avenue Association immediately opposed "motion" in display windows.[5]

In 1941, O'Clare was succeeded by Henry Callahan, one of the most famous of the display directors (fig. 33-10). His windows were (relatively) realistic vignettes with sophisticated mannequins which seemed to interact with each other— at luncheons, the theater, or while shopping (fig. 33-11). Professor Robert Hoskins of the Fashion Institute of Technology explains that Callahan moved to Saks Fifth Avenue in the late 1950s. In those much shallower display windows, he specialized in using startlingly simple designs, including "the Phantom," a headless mannequin that emphasized clothing.

During World War II, display windows were often creatively used for public service purposes (figs. 33-12, 33-13). Lord & Taylor devoted a great amount of space to this, and, in fact, still does to this day.

Skyscrapers on the Avenue

Until the 1920s, the avenue between Forty-second and Forty-ninth streets changed little. Homes had been either modified for use by trade or replaced by narrow commercial structures occupied by jewelers, milliners, and other exclusive businesses.

But during the frenzied construction of the late 1920s, most of the nineteenth-century "landmarks" were destroyed and replaced by towering paeans to commerce. The Hotel Bristol, Delmonico's, Temple Emanu-El, and Church of the Heavenly Rest disappeared. The patina of age, respectability and gentility—so cherished by earlier residents—disintegrated. Massive developments like the Empire State Building, Salmon Tower, Rockefeller Center, or even Tiffany & Co. changed the entire profile of the avenue. Church steeples became dwarfed by office buildings.

In 1927, James C. Young said, "[W]here the blue sky used to hang like a canopy, there are towers and buttresses of new and strange buildings. The saunterer who once carried every chimney in his memory finds the avenue so altered that he can scarcely recognize a landmark. . . ."[6]

The skyscrapers altered the streetscape and changed traffic patterns. But they still reinforced the notion that Fifth Avenue was for pedestrians. Often sheathed in limestone like the department stores and mansions, the buildings had setbacks which ensured that their heights didn't overwhelm the walkers. And the commercial buildings contained ground-floor stores. The rhythmically placed voids of the display windows set into limestone walls reinforced the avenue's human scale. Their presence also meant that there was always something to see on the street.

Traffic Troubles

Traffic remained an ever-worsening problem. The avenue was clogged with two-way traffic, double parking, and delivery vehicles from each store. In 1929, James Casey, the head of United Parcel Service, arrived from Seattle. From an office in the Chanin Building, he solicited stores which used their own delivery vehicles. Lord & Taylor and McCreery's were the first to use his service in 1930; within a year most of the stores were using it. Macy's was the last to join, in 1946. Using UPS vehicles allowed the stores to use their now-emptied basements for merchandise.

In 1920, an experimental wooden traffic tower on stilts was placed at Fifth

Overleaf
Fig. 35-1 The first bronze traffic signal tower at Forty-second and Fifth Avenue in 1922 is unveiled. The tower design was selected from 130 entries. Figures of eagles with outspread wings stood at the four corners of the light panels. The north and south faces contained illuminated clocks that struck at noon and midnight. Photo: Wide World Photos. Courtesy: Fifth Avenue Association

Fig. 36-1 This ca. 1936 view shows B. Altman's second-floor shoe salon, which had been recently modernized. Photo: Fay S. Lincoln. Courtesy: Historical Collections and Labor Archives, Penn State

Previous page
Fig. 35-2 View of Forty-second Street and Fifth Avenue taken from the New York Public LIbrary showing typical workday traffic in 1938. The neighborhood has become an office hub, and few elegant shops remain. Trolleys travel along Forty-second Street; the avenue still has two-way traffic. Courtesy: Municipal Archives, Department of Records and Information Services, City of New York

Avenue and Forty-second Street. It was replaced by one of seven beautiful bronze towers designed by architect Joseph H. Freedlander. More than 750 subscribers had donated $125,000 to have them erected between Washington Square and Fifty-ninth Street. The design, which had been selected from 130 entries, stood twenty-three feet high, rising from granite blocks. The red, amber, and green electric signals were operated by traffic policemen in the towers.

The master tower at 42nd Street was dedicated at ceremonies in December 1922 (fig. 35-1); the others were located at 14th, 26th, 34th, 50th, and 57th streets.

Just five years later, the police commissioner appealed to the Fifth Avenue Association to have them removed. The city objected because the towers used up roadway space and it was difficult to see the lights from the side streets without crowding the crosswalks. The *New York Times* editorialized, "The World thinks they are good-looking and altogether 'New Yorky.' "[7]

Despite a group of members who favored their retention, the Fifth Avenue Association offered to cooperate with the city to create a more efficient system. The association recommended that the new system include an amber warning light between the red and green signals "to give greater safety to pedestrians." The association also suggested that the new system be designed as "a creditable substitute for the bronze towers which have so distinctly marked Fifth Avenue."[8]

The city attempted to create a new system to speed midtown traffic and reduce congestion. To aid its evaluation, fifty "specially trained" traffic policemen distributed sixty thousand questionnaires to motorists to survey their routes, origins, and destinations.

The avenue's traffic towers were removed in 1929; overhead signals were used temporarily. In late 1930 the Board of Estimate and Apportionment approved 104 bronze traffic signal posts. Joseph H. Freedlander was again the designer (with "assistance" from the Board of Estimate). Each ten-foot post was surmounted by a one-foot-high figure of Mercury. Only Fifth Avenue was graced by these special standards, which were originally cast by Tiffany Studios. In 1931, they were placed between Eighth and Fifty-ninth streets at each intersection.

Loved by merchants, shoppers, and tourists, these ornamental standards remained until 1962. Traffic Commissioner Barnes, for whom the "Barnes Dance" pedestrian crossings were named, rejected the Fifth Avenue Association's requests to retain them. The city removed them as part of a program to replace "obsolete" signals with modern electronic ones.

In 1966, Fifth and Madison avenues were converted to one-way streets. Initially created to ease congestion during the transit strike, Fifth Avenue traffic was southbound and Madison Avenue traffic traveled northbound. More than two hundred city employees worked overnight to erect one-way traffic signs and repaint the street lines. Most of the merchants were delighted at what Walter Hoving termed the new "superhighway."

A series of "pedestrian-only" days started in the 1960s to aid holiday shopping; the avenue has also been closed on certain Sundays for street fairs and the annual book fair.

The Fifth Avenue Coach Company used open-air double-decked buses from 1907 until the 1930s. Sitting on the top was a marvelous and cheap date—ten cents each way starting at Washington Square. The regular double-decked buses disappeared in the 1950s. Aimless riding up and down the avenue came to an end (fig. 35-2). In the 1970s the city imported eight buses from England and tried to revive double-decked buses. Alas, the project was short-lived.

Entrenched Department Stores

Perhaps department stores did not have the rarefied atmosphere of the posh specialty stores. In those days Macy's was described as a "bazaar" with everything from books to peanuts sold on the main floor, and Bloomingdale's had not evolved into today's expensive emporium. Thirty-fourth Street contained a mixed group of stores.

So the avenue department stores which offered personal service, liberal

return policies, wide shopping aisles, and an atmosphere of calm civility were the best in the city. A Baltimore woman who used to come to New York City several times a year to shop remembers, "Before I would come to the city, I would call all my salesladies to let them know I was coming. They would have lots of things tucked away for me when I came in."

The respectable department stores remained so, but each one met the needs of different shoppers. The sporty Best & Co. shopper was never confused with the remarkably chic Bonwit Teller client. In fact, the cluster of lower Fifth Avenue stores were competitive with each other, as were the upper avenue shops. For example, in the 1930s, Lord & Taylor, Franklin Simon, Arnold Constable, and Russeks each sold

Fig. 36-3 View of a gift shop in B. Altman, ca. late 1920s. Courtesy: Collection of Professor Robert Hoskins

ensembles complete with proper accessories. Each store carried different lines, but since great quantities of the items were ordered, these outfits were particularly well-priced.

In efforts to "streamline" or "modernize," the department stores often stripped or covered the exquisite paneling, molding, marble and plaster ornamentation we now crave as a sign of "luxury" and "class." Bit by bit, through the years and continuing to this day, skylights are being covered and paneling is being ripped out.

B. Altman

B. Altman continued the department store tradition of carrying a bit of everything. The conservative customer felt comfortable on its sedate main floor; the stately store was not given to "fads."

The store had a very practical attitude; an entire floor became the "catalogue floor," which sold the reasonably priced merchandise featured in the seasonal catalogues. By 1930, with thoughts of innumerable Amelia Earharts flying the skies, it opened an aviation equipment department which featured clothing and accessories for aviatrixes, such as one-piece suits that couldn't "be ruined by the touch of nasty old engine grease." But its reputation was one of conservatism; a 1930 guide disparagingly described B. Altman's shoe department (fig. 36-1) as a place "where the potentates of the store have

unbent enough to permit the insidious note of modern decoration to creep in..."[9]

In 1927, the seventh floor was transformed into the Department of Interior Decoration with model rooms along the width of the Fifth Avenue frontage. Called "Casa Alta," the rooms ranged from a Spanish-tiled entrance hall to a French bedroom to an Early American bedroom. During its first week, the department attracted thousands of visitors.

In anticipation of the 1939 World's Fair crowds, B. Altman enlarged its selling space by filling in its rotunda (fig. 36-2). It added escalators as well. Even with the disappearance of the glorious leaded glass, the store was able to maintain its spacious ambiance by adding as few walls as possible. (fig. 36-3) In the late 1940s, the Charleston Garden, a double-height restaurant, was added on the eighth floor (fig. 36-4). Lined by a mural of a two-story plantation house on one wall and lush foliage on another, the space was filled with small tables holding removable trays. Despite the constant clatter of china and cutlery, it was a most ladylike place to have tea or lunch.

Into the 1950s and 1960s the store pampered the traditional grandmother but it encouraged her more stylish daughter to stay awhile. Along with expensive designer clothes and accessories, its variety of departments was a dizzying mix of the old-fashioned and the modern. Some, like the departments for fabrics or gourmet foods, seemed never to change. At the same time,

Fig. 36-4 The Charleston Garden restaurant was installed in B. Altman in the 1940s. Most of the other Fifth Avenue stores didn't have restaurants until then, or later. Courtesy: Collection of Ronda Wist

it had an elegant Charles of the Ritz hair salon; an antique map department; "Lotus Land," a shop of exotic Far Eastern items; and Studio 3, with off-beat and often exclusive items.

"It was like a country club," remembers a woman who worked there for twenty-nine years. "We weren't union, but we were one big family." She said that when she began in 1959, a hot meal was sold to the employees for twenty-five cents, and by the time the store closed, the price had risen to thirty-five cents. For every purchase of over one hundred dollars, staff received a fifty-percent discount. "The bosses were wonderful. Every six months they held a red rose breakfast to honor employees who had received complimentary letters from customers." Salespeople were trained for

several days before starting work. "We were told, 'The customer is your boss. Never point to the wrapping desk—take them.' " When she worked in the gift shop, one of its slower-moving items was a giant bird cage that cost $375. "After a customer bought it, the buyer was so overwhelmed that he bought me a huge bouquet of flowers."

The store continued on, with the avenue's kindest salespeople, roomiest aisles, and dependable merchandise. It was sold in 1985 and went through a peculiar modernization that sent its traditional customers fleeing and didn't attract any new ones. The landmarked building was granted a special permit to construct additional floors on the Madison Avenue side. Meanwhile, the store closed.

Everyone worried about the future

of this important building. But now its future looks secure: over 600,000 square feet will be occupied by the New York Resource Center—showrooms for interior furnishings, and 200,000 square feet will be the Science, Industry and Business Library of the New York Public Library. So Altman's will remain what it has always been—a "stately guardian."

Best & Co.

Best & Co., most famous for its children's departments, also became known for sporty clothing for women whose "goddess is Chanel." Clothing trends were ignored, and women could purchase their same favorites year after year. It specialized in practical classics like washable doeskin gloves. Departments changed with the seasons; a guide mentioned seeing "unfortunate models wandering about in snow-shoe costumes."

Philip LeBoutillier headed the store. From a family listed in the Social Register, he began his career as a delivery packer and became general manager in 1917. Considered an "individualist," he paid little attention to the competition and strongly supported women executives in retailing. He allowed buyers great flexibility to select the styles from clothing suppliers rather than requiring them to get approval from merchandising managers. In 1919, he set up one of the first pension plans for employees. An early proponent of branch stores, he opened the first suburban Best & Co. in Garden City, New York, in 1929.

"The whole theory of his operation of Best's was that everything must pay off handsomely. . . . Volume for its own sake never held any lure. . . . He was always interested primarily in net profit and his store showed the highest consistent profit record of any. . . . [Even in] 1933, Best's earned 3 percent on sales."

LeBoutillier asserted, "A retail store should be a suitable container and background for merchandise and nothing more. Pleasing to the eye, but not a monument . . . which generally doubles the cost."[10] In 1928, however, he added three stories to the building. In its press release the store cited research and surveys which had "deepened the company's opinion that the district would continue for years to be the greatest retail section in the world."[11]

Finally, in 1937, architect Harold Butterfield was hired to modernize the Best & Co. building, pargeting and simplifying the facade. Lewis Mumford thought it had evolved into "a good example

of an unobtrusive modern vernacular," and approved of much of the design including the Roman lettering above the entrance and the display window framing in metallic

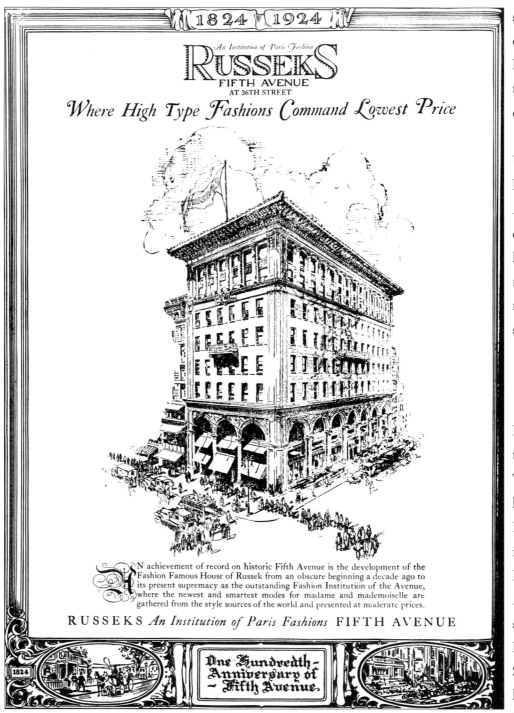

An Institution of Paris Fashion

RUSSEKS
FIFTH AVENUE
AT 36TH STREET

Where High Type Fashions Command Lowest Price

AN achievement of record on historic Fifth Avenue is the development of the Fashion Famous House of Russek from an obscure beginning a decade ago to its present supremacy as the outstanding Fashion Institution of the Avenue, where the newest and smartest modes for madame and mademoiselle are gathered from the style sources of the world and presented at moderate prices.

R U S S E K S *An Institution of Paris Fashions* F I F T H A V E N U E

One Hundredth Anniversary of Fifth Avenue

Fig. 36-5 A women's clothing shop had recently moved into the former Gorham Building after Gorham merged with Black, Starr & Frost and moved uptown. Russeks made few alterations to McKim, Mead & White's structure. Courtesy: Fifth Avenue Association

green. However, he deplored details like the retention of "motheaten" lintels and moldings on the upper floors: "The architect has made the wrong choices in those final details where a false motion spoils a good effect almost as completely as a streak of lipstick carried too far out of the general curve of the mouth can spoil a woman's face."[12]

Best & Co. remained at the West Thirty-fifth Street location until 1947. Afterward, the store was occupied by Bond's. The building was cleaned and renovated in 1980 and is now residential above ground-floor stores.

Russeks

In 1924, Russeks moved into the Gorham Building on Thirty-sixth Street. The store had been established by Frank and Isidore H. Russek in a small space on Eighteenth Street and Sixth Avenue in 1886. It specialized in fur accessories like muffs, and architect Stanford White brought his black broadcloth coats to be lined with mink there.

In 1913, the shop moved to a narrow store on Fifth

Avenue where David Nemerov worked as a window dresser for $25 a week. When the shop had moved uptown, it caught the attention of Max Weinstein, the head of an investment brokerage firm with offices at the Waldorf-Astoria. In 1924, he left his company to reorganize Russeks and became its president until 1947, when he was succeeded by Nemerov.

The store sold women's clothing and specialized in furs. In fact, Russeks had asserted that it had sold more furs than any other American store during World War II. It also had a fur wholesaling and manufacturing business, with its expensive furs sold under the Russeks label. The store advertised itself as "An Institution of Paris Fashions" (fig. 36-5). Its Paris design studio produced copies of French high-fashion dresses for "modest prices," with at most, ten copies of each model produced. The store's service was excellent. One war bride remembers having her wedding gown altered in one day.

Its window manne-quins were possibly Fifth Avenue's most notable: with

eyelashes of black embroidery thread, they were considered "amusing" and "alarming."

By the 1950s, the store began to suffer. In 1957 it was taken over by a group

Fig. 36-6 Franklin Simon was proud to be one of the first merchants to move to Fifth Avenue. Called "A Store of Individual Shops," his new store was considered a moderately priced version of Henri Bendel. Courtesy: Fifth Avenue Association

of Chicago investors. For the year ending March 1958, it had lost $127,000 on sales of $9 million. The store closed in 1959. After a disposal sale, the building was converted to offices. At the time of the closing, the Russeks fur salon in the Savoy-Hilton Hotel was enlarged.

In 1937, the seventy-nine-year-old Brick Presbyterian Church at the northwest corner of Thirty-seventh Street was sold, demolished and replaced by low-scale art deco buildings for A. S. Beck and The Lerner Shops.

Franklin Simon

During Franklin Simon's expansion in 1922, signs beneath the scaffolding assured customers "Continually showing New Fashions While Rebuilding The Individual Shops" (fig. 36-6). With space broken into different levels and elevators that opened in both directions, it seemed like a series of small, barely connected shops. It was described as a lower-priced version of Henri Bendel. A special entrance on Thirty-eighth Street led to the men's shop where American and English clothes were carried—it was the exclusive agent of Aquascutum coats.

Franklin Simon, a merchant much beloved by his employees and fellow retailers, died in 1934 at the age of sixty-nine. In the early years of the Depression, he had "preached a doctrine of optimism, counseling merchants that recovery would come ultimately and advising them not to adopt a 'trading down' policy . . . [because] too great concessions in price might induce customers, for many years to come, to seek low-priced good only."[13]

After a few years of decline, the business was sold by his widow to the Atlas Corporation. Prosperity returned with a president who had eight years of experience at Oppenheim Collins (on Thirty-fourth Street).

In the 1960s, Franklin Simon moved to the Thirty-fourth Street store vacated by Oppenheim Collins, and W. & J. Sloane moved to this building (fig. 36-7). With dim dustiness enveloping its beautiful furniture, the store and building ended their days. It was recently replaced by the 420 Fifth Avenue office building.

Across from Franklin Simon was Bonwit Teller, then an expensive but rather conservative store known for superb tailoring. The corset counter carried a wide array of "body gloves" made in their "Paris Studio," with corsets ranging from $50 to $175 (in 1930).

After Bonwit Teller's 1930 move to the corner of East Fifty-sixth Street, this building became known simply as 417 Fifth Avenue, an office building with ground-floor stores.

Lord & Taylor

"Everyone's always loved Lord & Taylor because the price is right and it had a very American atmosphere," recalls Eleanor Lambert. One world-weary shopper now says, "The only reason to get up early is to have coffee at Lord & Taylor." Coffee is served to early arrivals in the entrance vestibule as it has been since 1930. At 9:55 A.M., the National Anthem is played over the loudspeaker. The clock strikes 10:00 A.M., the doors open, and the shopping begins. This ritual perhaps epitomizes the store's appeal: It's very American and pays attention to the small details that improve the quality of one's shopping experience.

Lord & Taylor continued the grand department store tradition (figs. 36-8, 36-9). The store carried conservative clothing, but it had a consistently modern outlook. A 1930 shopping guide pronounced Lord & Taylor " a shop with the most leisurely charm that you will find this side [of] the Fifty-seventh Street Gold Coast."[14] Its wrapping service sent home packages that were carried in from elsewhere, even from Woolworth's. That charm was sorely tried in 1926, when a man disguised as a shopper stole an eight-foot-by-nine-foot tapestry, tucking it under his arm as he left the store through the employees' entrance. The tapestry was valued at $10,000 and dated from 1680.

After the 1925 Exposition des Arts Decoratifs in Paris, the Metropolitan Museum of Art and the Brooklyn Museum held extensive exhibits of Modernist furniture and decorative arts. However, a contemporary magazine noted that, "when it came to the point of introducing the mode to the casual, straying, shopping public, it has been the department stores that have actually done it."[15]

Beginning in 1925, Wannamaker's exhibited French modern furniture and a number of stores, including Macy's and Lord & Taylor, began to sell French contemporary furniture. Macy's, Wannamaker's, and Altman's exhibited modern American furniture in model rooms.

In 1928, Lord & Taylor went a step further. It presented a spectacular exposition of modern French decorative arts with displays of museum-quality furniture and accessories that were "purely educational" and not for sale (figs. 36-10, 36-11). The *New York Times* noted that the exhibition was epochal "in the sense not of creating but marking an epoch."[16] Dorothy Shaver, then a "director," had spent six months looking for pieces in Europe and ultimately assembled the entire collection in France.

Nine rooms were decorated with furniture by Chareau, Sue et Mare, Dunand, and Ruhlmann, fabrics by Rodier, rugs designed by Léger and Lurcat, crystal

Fig. 36-7 View of the west side of Fifth Avenue from West Thirty-seventh street, ca. late 1970s. After Franklin Simon moved to West Thirty-fourth Street, the building was occupied by W. & J. Sloane. The large sign for the Lerner Shops covers two art deco storefronts. The entire block has been razed and replaced by the 420 Fifth Avenue building. Courtesy: New York City Department of City Planning

accessories by Baccarat, and silver by Puiforcat. Store president Samuel Reyburn claimed that one of the reasons for the show was "to determine whether the American public is really interested in the new."[17] In the exhibition catalogue, he offered to present an American exhibition in the future if public interest warranted it. In fact, later that year, Lord & Taylor opened a Department of Modern Design and sold American versions of the French art deco furniture.

The furniture departments experienced a downturn during World War II, so the store opened an "antiques" section which displayed antiques and old furniture priced between five and five thousand dollars. Considered a solution to the furniture problem of "wartime budgets," the department tagged and reduced all items by 10 percent each week. People could anonymously dispose of home furnishings through the department.

After Samuel Reyburn's retirement in 1936, Walter Hoving served as president from 1936 to 1945; Dorothy Shaver was president from 1946 until her death in

1959. Shaver, who had begun her career in the comparison shopping bureau, "was absolutely fabulous" said Robert Hoskins. "She's acknowledged as the restorer of the store's panache—she is credited with marvelous little tricks that make all the difference. She filled the store with red roses, which became its symbol, hung green awnings to announce spring's arrival, opened a college shop and presented red felt cushions for customers to rest their elbows while trying on gloves."

Women's garments were sold on many floors throughout the building, and it was tiring to coordinate ensembles. That defect was remedied with designer Raymond Loewy's 1937 remodeling. This entailed systems

Fig. 36-8 This view shows the main floor of Lord & Taylor, ca. 1930s. At this time, the interior retained its original decorative finishes, chandeliers, and display cases. It's interesting to see that "Bridge and Games" rated a counter on the main floor. Photo: Worsinger. Courtesy: Collection of Professor Robert Hoskins

Fig. 36-9 Lord & Taylor elves install Christmas decorations, after hours, ca. late 1940s. Courtesy: Collection of Professor Robert Hoskins

Fig. 36-10 This window contains a selection from Lord & Taylor's remarkable 1928 exposition of art deco furniture. Photo: Worsinger. Courtesy: Collection of Professor Robert Hoskins

a women's budget department with sections for hats, suits, dresses, and shoes.

Space, still in abundance, was more rigidly defined. Semicircular seating, rounded edges, and asymmetrical arrangement of small units all helped to create the "illusion of privacy."

Although the store contemplated a move to Fifth Avenue and Fifty-second Street in 1944, it remained in place, and opened suburban stores. Credited with introducing the "American Look," Lord & Taylor helped to propel Claire McCardell, Bonnie Cashin, Pauline Trigère, and Vera Maxwell to fame (figs. 36-12, 36-13, 36-14). At the same time, the store sold many French designs, and had exclusive Hermes and Liberty of London lines.

Finally in 1934, the Wendel house, at the

modernization (including ventilation), reconfiguring and redistributing departments, and creating new departments.

The fourth floor, which had originally held a multitude of departments including the children's barber shop, French hats, automobile apparel, and boys' clothing, now held "various kinds of women's apparel." Women's shoes were moved to the fourth floor from the second floor where they had been with children's shoes. The sixth floor, which had sold furniture and blankets, became devoted to youngsters, with everything from layettes to clothing for college students. A new department, the Men's Budget Shop, was placed on the tenth floor, which had previously been occupied by restaurants, cigars and candy. The second floor became

Fig. 36-11 This window displays rugs selected from Lord & Taylor's 1928 exposition of art deco furniture. Photo: Worsinger. Courtesy: Lord & Taylor

36-12

Fig. 36-14 This 1961 window displays American designer Bonnie Cashin's coats, which transcend time. Note that the department store windows often displayed additional shoes, purses, and jewelry to accessorize the exhibited clothing. Photo: Nick Malan. Courtesy: Lord & Taylor

Fig. 36-12 Lord & Taylor credited itself with coining the term "The American Look." This 1950s window displays sportswear by Claire McCardell, one of America's most innovative designers. Photo: Worsinger. Courtesy: Lord & Taylor

Fig. 36-13 This 1949 window display salutes Pauline Trigvère, after she won the American Fashion Critics award. Courtesy: Collection of Professor Robert Hoskins

36-13

140

Within the image:

LORD & TAYLOR
FASHION
PREMIÈRE

A Bonnie Cashin coat
stops the show.

who else combines leather, suede,
furs and wools
with such dazzling imagination!

Her collection in the
Country Clothes Shop, Sports Wear, Fifth

36-14

Fig. 36-18 View of east side of the avenue from Thirty-ninth Street. This photograph shows the art deco Woolworth's, Arnold Constable, and the corner of Lane Bryant. Woolworth's, which replaced the Union League Club, and Lane Bryant have been demolished. Arnold Constable closed in 1975. The building is now occupied by the Mid-Manhattan Library. Courtesy: New York City Department of City Planning

northwest corner of Thirty-ninth Street, was demolished. The odd, shuttered house with its bare side yard had been pointed out by tour guides; it was sitting on some of the city's most valuable property (fig. 36-15). Ironically, it was replaced by a five-and-dime store. Architect Edward F. Sibbert designed a nine-story (plus penthouse) building for S. H. Kress & Co. The store leased the property from Drew University, one of the major legatees under the will of the last surviving Wendel (fig. 36-16).

The city's most elegant dime store was designed to maximize efficiency in a kind of machine for selling. The lower floors offered more than thirty-five hundred items for sale which confronted the shopper in neatly displayed piles (fig. 36-17). Lunch counters had sunken service floors for waiters; the upper floors were used for storage to minimize the time required to supply additional merchandise to the selling floors.

Architectural Forum considered the design to be "a smoothly functioning organism, devoted to the selling of small articles in fantastic quantities and at a staggering rate of speed, it is perhaps the most interesting building of its kind ever erected, something less than that as an architectural design."[18]

With minimal personal service offered, all of the space was devoted to display and sale. The main floor had no columns. Illuminated numbers on bronze standards delineated aisle numbers. Direct and indirect lighting combined to create a brightness level "more than six times the brightness of the average department store interior. High-intensity lighting is stimulating, and its effect on the buying urge is greater than is commonly realized." This five and ten cent store made every effort to be worthy of its Fifth Avenue address. Its floors were travertine, its walls were burled wood, and its staircases had railings of brass. It was a grand space where everyone could enjoy spending their dimes.

The limestone building was ultimately demolished for the Republic National Bank building.

In 1929, the Union League Club announced its removal to the heart of Murray Hill, at Park Avenue and Thirty-seventh Street. A few years later, its site was occupied by an art moderne F. W. Woolworth & Co.

In the 1930s, a number of stores were constructed; despite being sheathed in art deco finery, A. S. Beck, Kress, and Woolworth offered modestly priced merchandise and reflected the decline in the economy and the downturn of the avenue below Forty-second Street.

Arnold Constable

Next to Woolworth's, Arnold Constable merged with Stewart and Company in 1925, with Isaac Liberman as the head of the new organization. He authorized an addition to the Fifth Avenue frontage, and opened their first branch store in New Rochelle in 1937 (fig. 36-18).

Despite a very traditional reputation, with Eleanor Roosevelt as perhaps its most famous customer, the store was also known for wonderful, inexpensive silk underwear. Each Thursday was Bridal Day in the French Room. During Easter and Christmas holidays, the College Corner was staffed by college students who dispensed wardrobe and other advice.

In 1929, to celebrate the 102nd anniversary of the store's founding, Arnold Constable & Co. held an exhibition depicting Fifth Avenue's growth from a dirt road to the present. In addition to old photographs and drawings, were paintings, drawings, and etchings by such artists as Childe Hassam and John Sloane.

Many families had charge accounts for generations. Through the years, Arnold Constable remained a staid department store that never seemed crowded. Liberman retired as chairman in 1967, but his nephew Merwin Bayer remained as president. By the early 1970s, the store consolidated and the Mid-Manhattan branch of the New York Public Library occupied the upper three floors. By 1974, Arnold Constable occupied the main floor only. The next year, the store reported a "small operating profit" on sales of $5 million, but decided to concentrate on a chain of small suburban stores instead. The store closed and the Mid-Manhattan Library took over the building. A small gift shop operated by the Metropolitan Museum of Art occupies the corner of the main floor.

Peck & Peck

Peck & Peck began as a hosiery store on Madison Square in 1887 (fig. 36-19). After vacating the site for the construction of the Flatiron Building, the store continued to move north along Fifth Avenue. By the late 1920s it had several branches and carried sportswear and accessories as well. In its early days, it was one of the few stores that carried black stockings that were colorfast. Imported from Germany and hand embroidered by firemen waiting for a fire, the stockings were dyed in the United States. The store also carried $500 silk stockings with handmade lace inserts, for customers such as Lillian Russell and Theda Bara. In 1916, Peck & Peck became the first New York store to open a resort shop in Palm Beach.

When men began wearing socks to match their ties, the store expanded its lines. When the tie manufacturer brought over some silk sweaters, women wanted them, with skirts to match. So the store launched its sportswear lines. By the 1930s it carried smart "career girl" type fashions. The manufacturer of Betmar Hats, which supplied hats to Best &

Co., Lord & Taylor, and Peck & Peck, among others, recalls that, "Peck & Peck sent plaid fabric to our New Jersey factory so we could make hats to match the store's suits."

Its store at 585 Fifth Avenue (extant, lower-floor alterations), designed by G. A. and H. Boehm, used two kinds of colored marble for the lower three stories. (fig. 36-20)

Fig. 36-19 A 1957 advertisement for Peck & Peck, which specialized in sportswear and accessories. Courtesy: Seymour Durst

Lane Bryant

In 1947, a ten-story building for Lane Bryant opened at Fortieth Street and Fifth Avenue. The store had begun when Lena Bryant, a young widow, began to specialize

in creating maternity gowns for her clients. On her first bank deposit, she mistakenly wrote "Lane" rather than "Lena" and the name stuck. In 1911, the *New York Herald* accepted the first advertisement for maternity apparel. Its building was demolished, but the store recently moved back to the avenue, in the Republic National Bank Building which replaced S. H. Kress.

Men on the Avenue

The jumble of nineteenth century relics around Forty-second Street was demolished in the late 1920s. The older buildings were replaced by skyscrapers with ground-floor banking rooms, continuing the hustle and bustle of the Grand Central Terminal district.

Fifth Avenue, long the embodiment of wealth, now became the obvious symbol of money. Banks were everywhere. Society's sentimental writers bemoaned banks

Overleaf
Fig. 36-20 This photograph was taken in 1927 to show unsightly signs. Peck & Peck occupies 587 Fifth Avenue. Courtesy: Fifth Avenue Association

replacing Delmonico's and Sherry's. The four corners of Forty-fourth Street, previously society's social center, were occupied by banks. (They remain so, but with different banks.) A number of restaurants moved to Fifth Avenue, but the center of fashionable eating had shifted east. While Schrafft's and Childs opened near the stores and offices, the tony restaurants opened on Park Avenue.

During the Depression, failures of financial institutions like S. W. Strauss, the Bank of US, and the Harriman Bank left quite a few vacancies on the avenue. However, throughout the 1930s, the avenue maintained numerous branches north of Forty-second Street. Bankers Trust was at the southeast corner of Forty-second Street; in 1935 it moved into space vacated by the Harriman National Bank at the southeast corner of Forty-fourth Street (fig. 37-1). It leased the space from the Dry Dock Savings Institution which had taken the property in foreclosure. Shreve, Lamb & Harmon extensively remodeled the bank at an estimated cost of $300,000. Manufacturers Trust Company was at Forty-third and Fifty-fifth streets, the Fifth Avenue Bank and Guaranty Trust Company was at Forty-fourth Street, the Central Mercantile Bank was in the Delmonico Building, the Empire Trust Company was at Forty-seventh Street, the Colonial Trust Company was at Fifty-second Street, Chemical Bank was at Fifty-fourth Street, and the New York Trust Company was at Fifty-seventh Street.

In the 1940s, banks were joined by airlines offices which began to fill spaces previously occupied by stores. The area north of Forty-second Street was bitterly dubbed "Airline Alley." Air France was believed to be the first airline office to open on the avenue in 1946. By the end of the 1950s, there were twenty-two offices on the avenue.

In a perfect illustration of the avenue's metamorphosis, Iberia Airlines moved into a building which had once been a home, and altered at the turn of century for the budding Henri Bendel. In 1972, as part of the City Planning Commission's Fifth Avenue Special District designed to reinforce the avenue's retail character, certain spaces, like airline offices and banks were limited to 15 percent of a building's ground floor space. So, airline offices requiring additional space had to move off the avenue.

As office workers crowded the section around Forty-second Street, the women's clothing and accessory shops moved north. Men's stores and clubs had already consolidated in the Forties. The side streets and Madison Avenue continued to house male institutions like Abercrombie & Fitch, Tripler & Co., Brooks Brothers, Wetzel (men's tailors), and the Yale Club.

Fifth Avenue also catered to men. Alfred Dunhill and Sulka & Co. shared the

Fig. 37-1 During the Depression, Bankers Trust Company moved from Forty-second Street and Fifth Avenue into this building. Renovation of this space cost $300,000. Courtesy: Bankers Trust Company

ground floor of a building at 512-514 Fifth Avenue. Sulka's most inexpensive ready-made shirts were $10, while for example, B. Altman charged $7.50 for a custom-made evening shirt. So potential Sulka shoppers were advised, "If you want the most exquisite quality and are willing to pay for it. . . . "[19] In 1937, Sulka moved to the former Kurzman Building at 661 Fifth Avenue, into space remodeled at a cost of two-hundred-thousand dollars.

Budd, at 572 Fifth Avenue (extant, ground-floor alterations) since 1909, had been founded in 1861. In the 1930s it continued to be run by the founder's descendants. Although it carried ready-made shirts and pajamas, most of its orders were for custom work. Wallach Brothers moved to Forty-fifth Street, a block above Weber and Heilbroner; Broadstreets operated on Forty-seventh Street; Browning, King was on Forty-fifth Street and John David was at Forty-third Street. AG Spalding & Brothers sold sporting goods at 523 Fifth Avenue and after the Lefcourt Building needed the site, it moved to 518 Fifth Avenue. Until 1955, it sold "anything that the most adventurous sports man could possibly require, including bicycles." The store featured a resident polo specialist.

Finchley's, a men's clothier, moved from 5 East Forty-sixth Street to 564 Fifth Avenue. On the site of a women's clothing

Fig. 37-2 View of the west side of Fifth Avenue from Forty-sixth Street, ca. 1970s. The former Finchleys still has its English Tudor trim. Chock Full o'Nuts occupies the former Budd store. Courtesy: New York City Department of City Planning

shop, architect Beverly King designed a building with a north tower and "half-timber" trim (actually fireproof composition because of fire codes) (fig. 37-2). The British appearance reflected the British-sounding name. This store disguised as a home was intended to make men feel comfortable.

Service was the key, particularly for men. Many department stores sold men's clothing on the most accessible floor—the main one—and Lord & Taylor, for instance, had an express elevator to the men's floor.

Finchley's Edmund Goodman, the head of the firm, personally welcomed each customer and directed him to a salesman. The customer was accompanied through the store by the salesman, who helped him with all of his purchases.

The first floor held different salesrooms with built-in ebony display cases for hats, shoes, neckwear, and collars and shirts. The second through fourth floors held other clothing; the fifth floor held the college club room with a piano, fireplace and "current literature scattered about on the tables."

Fifth Avenue
As Office Hub

Somehow, the northeast corner of Forty-second Street had been overlooked until recently. It held Levi Morton's former home—where Edith Jones Wharton had made her debut into New York Society in 1879. The commercially occupied building remained until 1990 when it was demolished for a future office building.

For the most part, many older buildings had outlived their usefulness on the avenue. The low-rise buildings looked like elderly midgets at a convention of young basketball players. Not only were the buildings out of scale, but the city's socially acceptable areas were distinctly demarcated. And this area had lost its cachet as the center of fashionable activities. But it was perfect for high-priced office space. The real estate values had escalated astronomically; building owners must have felt that they had won the lottery by sitting on their property.

The properties were sold in the 1920s, but as Seymour Durst remarked, "Most of the large office buildings opened just in time for the Depression." Not surprisingly, the Vanderbilts and other property owners sold their parcels in the mid-1920s. In 1930, the Fifth Avenue Association announced a very low vacancy rate in the ground floors of the avenue buildings. But Mr. Durst remembers, "With all that construction, there was a 25 percent vacancy rate for office space on the avenue. . . . The office market really didn't come back until after the war."

The Waldorf-Astoria was still a superb meeting place, but it really had not aged well. The newer, posher hotels were uptown or on Park Avenue. Since it was in the heart of the retail district, however, the hotel's ground floor space on the Thirty-fourth Street side was converted to shops in 1925. But they didn't last long. As Nathan Silver explained in *Lost New York*, "The old Waldorf-Astoria met its end in a typical New York way: since the entire block was already under one ownership, it was cheaper for the builders of the future Empire State Building to buy it than try to acquire nearby property piecemeal."[20]

John Jacob Raskob met Alfred E. Smith during the Governor's abortive attempt to run against Herbert Hoover. In 1928, after the election, Raskob hired Smith to be the "front man" for his proposed Empire State Building project.

After sixteen attempts, architect William Lamb of Shreve, Lamb & Harmon, came up with the basic design, which was far more streamlined than the contemporaneous "wedding cake" skyscrapers. From the street line, the base rose to the fifth floor; above that soared the tower. The elegantly detailed limestone base, with a ribbon of storefronts framed in black granite, continued the low scale of Fifth Avenue. The avenue entrance was flanked by monumental columns crowned by stylized animal motifs. The soaring tower contained pairs of windows framed in dull red aluminum and vertically joined by metal spandrels (fig. 38-1).

Looking for a way to make the Empire State Building the tallest, higher than the Chrysler Building's eighty-five stories, Smith announced that a dirigible mooring mast would loom above the eighty-sixth floor. This two-hundred-foot tower, barely used of course, brought the building's height to 1,250 feet—clearly taller than the Chrysler Building's 1,046 feet.

The two-story marble lobby had a number of bridges at the second level (since enclosed). The Fifth Avenue entrance led to a gigantic marble panel with a metallic rendering of the building (fig. 38-2).

During the Waldorf-Astoria's demolition in October 1929, construction workers discovered a locked subbasement that held the still-full wine cellar of Mrs. Astor. Excavation work went on around the clock and the building went up in record time. Lewis Hine's photographs of the steelworkers high in the sky, like those on Rockefeller Center's RCA Building and any of the other skyscrapers, make one weep. It is still scary to see the photographs of these poor, ill-shod men, risking their lives for the appreciated Depression-era jobs.

The building opened in May 1931 with a grand ribbon-cutting ceremony. President Hoover pressed a button from Washington, D.C., that lit up the tower. However, the building was only half-rented, and was nicknamed the "Empty State Building."

Difficulty renting space was not its only problem. Migrating birds flew against its walls, suicides found a wonderful pinnacle, and in 1945, the war "made its greatest impact on Fifth Avenue," said Durst. A B-25 bomber lost its way and crashed into the building's seventy-ninth floor. Fourteen people were killed and twenty-six were injured.[21] The building burned, and survived, to become an icon of the city.

The Bristol Hotel had long before become the Bristol Building, occupied by small offices and ground-floor stores. Its Forty-second Street frontage was usually covered by a large billboard. The development site was waiting for a development. It was demolished for builder Walter J. Salmon's fifty-eight-story tower. In December 1930, before the formal opening of his building, Salmon admitted that, "it will take some time to absorb the approximately 500,000 square feet of office space . . . but the enterprise was undertaken with the greatest faith in the future of midtown expansion and development. Today Forty-second Street and Fifth Avenue is the very center of the world's greatest retail district, affording one of the greatest purchasing powers on the globe, through the thousands of potential buyers who pass through it daily."[22] Ground-floor retail space was so important that the first floor facade was virtually all plate glass windows and shop entrances. Seventeen stores were planned for the Forty-second Street frontage and four for Fifth Avenue, including the corner store. Despite the creation of the five-day workweek, the building was half

Opposite
Fig. 38-1 A view of the Empire State Building, when it was the world's tallest. This soaring structure and Rockefeller Center were built during the Depression, giving thousands work and the city hope. Courtesy: Empire State Building

Fig. 38-2 A 1930s view shows the Empire State Building's Fifth Avenue lobby entrance with its rendering in marble and metal. Photo: Fay S. Lincoln. Courtesy: Historical Collections and Labor Archives, Penn State

about to gild these turrets for the last time. The tides of the avenue are about to engulf the temple as they have swept away so many notable buildings."[23]

It seemed miraculous that the exotic Saracenic minarets, now completely surrounded by commerce, had lasted as long as they had. Congregation Emanu-El merged with Temple Beth-El and replaced the home of Mrs. William Astor at East Sixty-fifth Street. The congregation sold its site for over $6 million to Benjamin Winter, a developer. He had been accused of driving the Astors and Vanderbilts from Fifth Avenue because he purchased their homes and replaced them with skyscrapers which he believed were "America's first contribution to the art of the world."

Winter sold the site to Joseph Durst. In 1927, while Durst was demolishing the temple, Abraham E. Lefcourt proposed to pay him $370 per square foot for the property (fig. 38-3). Lefcourt paid this high price because "he had wanted all his life to own a corner on Fifth Avenue."[24] Known as the Lefcourt-National Building, 521 Fifth Avenue at forty stories and five hundred feet high was

completed in eighty-eight working days. Over one thousand men were employed at the peak of the construction.

Affluent congregations of the houses of worship had already moved to more fashionable uptown neighborhoods. And Temple Emanu-El, with its Saturday morning services, had another problem: The noise from the street intruded upon their Sabbath services. When it was sold, the *New York Times* mourned, "The sun is

Opposite
Fig. 38-3 View toward Fifth Avenue during the 1926 demolition of the exotic Temple Emanu-El. Construction workers—or scavengers—stand atop the arches, possibly gathering small pieces of the building, which were given away as souvenirs. Facing Fifth Avenue, to the north of the synagogue, is Sherry's. Courtesy: Congregation Emanu-El of the City of New York

then Fifth Avenue's tallest. Designed by Shreve, Lamb & Harmon, the building was Fifth Avenue's first in which the five setbacks and tower were in the center of the building, giving the avenue frontage a symmetrical elevation.

Whyte's, an old New York restaurant, moved uptown into this building from the financial district to their new half-million dollar space. Considered the one place to get "real American food," it also offered dancing each night from 6:30 to 9:30 P.M. and tea on Saturdays.

Lefcourt, a former garment center employee, took advantage of the financial angles the optimistic 1920s had to offer. While his building was under construction, he formed a holding company for a number of his buildings and offered 100,000 shares to the public. Within a few years, he opened the Lefcourt Normandie Bank and sold stocks through his Normandie National Securities.

His bank failed. Lefcourt had to repay outstanding loans to the soon-to-fail Bank of US. Many of his buildings were constructed on leased property and he was in arrears on his payments.

On a Tuesday in 1932, stockholders began a suit against Lefcourt and an associate. By Sunday morning he was dead, at his home in the Savoy-Plaza, after his third heart attack in one week. His funeral was held at the new Temple Emanu-El.

In 1919 the Guaranty Trust Company took over the leases held by Louis Sherry on his building on Forty-fourth Street. Cross and Cross designed the eleven-story building and Ricci and Zari designed the sliding bronze doors weighing six-hundred-plus pounds leading to the grand banking room. The Forty-fourth Street entrance led to rooms for women customers, including a reception room with antique oak paneling and a marble fireplace. The basement's safe deposit vaults numbered ten thousand with provision made for an additional five thousand. The space they vacated after three years, in architectural firm York and Sawyer's Postal Life Building, was taken by the Columbia Bank, which moved from 507 Fifth Avenue.

Delmonico's closed in 1923, "suffering the effects" of Prohibition, and was not demolished until 1925. The real estate was optimal for offices. And the restaurant's clients were at best, moving uptown, or at worst, dead. Standing in the residue of the demolished building, F. S. Laurence noted the perfect condition of the terra-cotta of the twenty-nine-year-old building. Describing its "dignified restraint and mellow, unostentatious richness, which was steadying to the mind in the surrounding scramble of towering, sky-piercing structures which have begun to shut in 'The Avenue' during the past ten years. Perhaps its color was one explanation of this. The soft, deep yellow buff of its brick and terra-cotta facade was as grateful to the sense as the permeating warmth of a glass of old wine in the far-off days when governments were human."[25]

The Harriman Building rose on the site. At 430 feet high, it was—for a short while—the neighborhood's tallest building. Architect H. Craig Severance's design of limestone and buff brick quietly and tastefully clad the building that held the executive offices of the Bank of US, an erratic operation that made substantial loans to real estate friends.

The Church of the Heavenly Rest moved uptown and the adjacent old buildings vacated. On their site rose a skyscraper with exotic polychromy accentuated by its buff-colored neighbors. The Fred F. French Building housed the corporate headquarters of Fred Fillmore French's company, which he had established when he was twenty-seven, in 1910. One of French's famous comments was, "You can't overbuild New York," certainly an apt motto for the 1920s.

This building offers one of the city's most encompassing architectural experiences. The entrance vestibules and vaulted lobby have polychromed ceilings, bronze doors, marble walls, crystal chandeliers—a profusion of colors and textures (fig. 38-4). Every interior surface is covered by bronze or colored motifs that amaze one with the workmanship and attention to detail.

In 1921, French created the "French Plan," a type of cooperative investment, based on "making a small profit on a large business as opposed to large profits on a small business."[26] Without inflating costs, the French Plan made money by handling various aspects of the development through different companies, but joined under one president. After site acquisition by the Fred F. French Investing Co., a building was designed by the Fred F. French Co., Architects & Builders. The investing company underwrote and sold stock for the new building, which was constructed by the Fred F. French Construction Co., and upon completion, it was managed by the Fred F. French Management Co. Until that time, the "French Plan" had been used for residential projects, notably Tudor City, which had begun in 1925.

The Fred F. French Building was designed by the firm of Sloan and Robertson, as well as by H. Douglas Ives, the French Company's in-house chief architect. Ives was quoted as saying the architectural style was "Mesopotamian." The Landmarks Preservation Commission designation report is a bit more specific by considering it a "proto-Art Deco design with strong Near Eastern influences."

The French Building rose thirty-eight stories to a height of 416 feet. The three-story limestone base supports a burnt orange brick midsection rising to the eleventh floor. Above this a series of setbacks, emphasized by horizontal black ornamentation, culminate in a tower surmounted by a three-story penthouse. The building is rumored to have been constructed by the first building construction crew of Caughnawaga Indians from Canada.[27]

Designed as the company's calling card, its ornamentation is most apparent on the bronze detailed base and on the polychromed tower. The ground floor's row of continuous storefronts (originally with recessed central entrances), is interrupted by one entrance on Fifth Avenue and the main entrance on Forty-fifth Street. The storefronts are surmounted by an Egyptianized bronze frieze of winged Assyrian beasts separated by lotus and papyrus stalks. The bronze entrance arches, delineated by a continuous motif of lotus and papyrus, are set below spandrels containing, on the left, a stylized male holding a column, compass and two T-squares, and on the right, a female holding a beehive (a symbol of industry). The Fifth Avenue entrance leads to an outer vestibule with a vaulted ceiling of polychromed animals; the vestibule on Forty-fifth Street is enclosed. H. D. Ives told the *New York Times*, in 1927, that the building's motifs combined ancient symbols with modern interpretation: "From the beginnings of architecture down through Roman, Romanesque and Gothic periods, the use for which buildings were intended was expressed by symbols, and so in the French Building we have endeavored in the panels at the top of the tower to express not only the purpose for which the building is to be

Fig. 38-4 The entrance vestibule of the "Mesopotamian" Fred F. French Building, constructed on the site of the Church of the Heavenly Rest. Photo: Carl Forster. Courtesy: New York City Landmarks Preservation Commission

38-5

38-6

used, commerce, but the character and activities of our own organization, the Fred F. French Companies. The central motif of the large panels on the north and south sides is a rising sun, progress, flanked on either side by two winged griffons, integrity and watchfulness. At either end are two beehives with golden bees, the symbol of industry." (figs. 38-5, 38-6).

The French companies were located in offices on the twelfth and thirteenth floors. Each morning at 9:00 A.M., Fred F. French gave an inspirational talk to his employees in the auditorium.

In 1921, I. Miller opened on the site of florist Thorley's "House of Flowers," an old building with floral decorations protruding from every aperture. The building, a sentimental favorite, was replaced by Warren and Wetmore's narrow twelve-story office building at 562 Fifth Avenue. (Thorley moved to Mrs. Russell Sage's former house next to the Collegiate Church of St. Nicholas.)

Opposite
Fig. 38-5 View of the recently restored Fred F. French building's tower. The rising sun (progress) is flanked by winged griffons (integrity and watchfulness). The beehives with golden bees symbolize industry. Photo: Diane Kaese.

Fig. 38-6 Winged Assyrian beasts separated by lotus and papyrus stalks surmount the bronze entrance arch. The spandrels of the arch are ornamented with a stylized male holding a column, compass, and two T-squares, and a female holding a beehive. Photo: Carl Forster. Courtesy: New York City Landmarks Preservation Commission

Miller sold shoes on three floors, including a basement department known as "Corner of Paris." Here, shoes by designer Andre Perugia were sold—which helped to establish his international reputation. Israel Miller also brought back to America Perugia's "sun tan" stockings, considered revolutionary, because all stockings were white, black, or dark brown. I. Miller served tea each afternoon and cigarettes "were on the house." In 1928, another I. Miller opened at Fortieth Street and in 1941 a third shop opened in the Aeolian Building.

In 1938, after a lifetime filled with good works, Helen Gould Shepard died. Her husband died in 1942 and the house at 579 Fifth Avenue became a sort of pathetic second-hand shop. In the 1950s, it was replaced by a building described as having the effect of an eleven-story building resting on a sheet of glass. The architectural firm of Emory Roth & Sons designed it and the similar building erected on the corner of Forty-eighth Street, the site of Robert Goelet's home.

In 1920, Robert Goelet commissioned John H. Duncan to design a two-story art gallery at the vacant lot at 606 Fifth Avenue. His mother, Mary Rita Wilson (sister of Grace Vanderbilt and Marshall Orme) and widow of Ogden Goelet, lived in the Goelet house next door at 608 Fifth Avenue until her death in 1929. That year, several sales of the contents of her house were held; in 1930 the house and the gallery were demolished.

Goelet commissioned a building of

Vermont verde antique and white Dover cream marble that complimented the Rockefeller Center buildings across the street. The ten-story building was specifically designed for retail uses on the lower floors and offices above. Although this often turned out to be the case not by design, the engineer Edward H. Faile and his associate, Victor L. S. Hafner, actually designed a building that worked well for both uses. To ensure uninterrupted show windows for the retail space, Faile designed a cantilevered third-story resting on two-story-high columns, which are recessed five feet from the building line. The marble and bronze lobby is a small work of art filled with various configurations of the Goelet crest—the swan—above entwined G's.

In 1964 the structure was remodeled for the Swiss Center. The main entrance and retail space was altered. However, the entrance arch at 4 West Forty-ninth Street remains.

Rockefeller Center

By the late 1920s, the houses on the side streets of Columbia University's "upper estate" had deteriorated and the Fifth Avenue frontage was commercial, housing DePinna and Brill Brothers, in addition to other stores (fig. 39-1).

The Metropolitan Opera Company, located at Thirty-ninth Street and Broadway, was looking for larger quarters in a more elegant neighborhood. To make the move

39-1

financially feasible, John D. Rockefeller Jr. stepped in and agreed to lease the University's twelve acres. The Opera House was to be in the center of a development of office buildings known as Metropolitan Square. Rockefeller intended to share costs with the Opera House and other developers of commercial buildings. Just after the 1929 Stock Market crash, the Opera withdrew and decided to remain on Broadway. Rockefeller remained with the site and in 1931 the project was renamed Rockefeller Center.

So during the Depression, construction began on the world's largest privately owned business and entertainment center. And New York was grateful. Not only was this project going to help revitalize the economy, it was also going to anchor the exclusive shopping district. As the Columbia properties had protected the integrity of the Vanderbilt Colony, Rockefeller Center was going to reinforce the high standards of Fifth Avenue. The original project (subsequently enlarged) included fourteen buildings encompassing five million square feet of rentable space. Approximately seventy-five thousand workers were employed on site (figs. 39-2, 39-3).

The project architects—Reinhard &

Hofmeister; Corbett, Harrison and MacMurray; and Hood and Fouilhoux—designed the complex as a fantastic city-within-a-city.

The complex was planned to benefit tenants, pedestrians, patrons, and even vehicular traffic. The central placement of the tallest building prevents the pedestrian from becoming overwhelmed by height or submerged in continuous shadow. The T-shaped open space nurtures the pedestrian activities amid the limestone facades. Rockefeller Plaza, a midblock street parallel to Fifth Avenue, facilitates circulation. The entertainment buildings face Sixth Avenue nearest the theater district. Subterranean passageways increased pedestrian circulation. Every building is ornamented with sculpture, murals, mosaics. The art is an integral part of the architecture, not just an afterthought. The complex is a marvel (fig. 39-4).

After the Sixth Avenue "Radio Buildings" were planned, the designs for the Fifth Avenue frontage had still not become final. The resulting low-scale buildings related superbly to Fifth Avenue. The difficulty of obtaining tenants was obviated when French and English consortiums signed leases for the buildings between Forty-ninth and Fifieth streets. The landscaped passage between them, leading back to the sunken plaza and the Prometheus fountain, was aptly named "the Channel Gardens." It has turned out to be one of Manhattan's most enduring and refreshing oases.

A similar grouping, the six-story Palazzo d'Italia and International Building North, are across West Fiftieth Street. They, however, project as wings to the recessed forty-one story International Building (figs. 39-5, 39-6).

The limestone International buildings, nearly identical in massing, differ in sculpture and ornamentation. Each rises five stories with a lateral setback at the sixth floor. With the precise detailing and judicious use of art, the buildings relate to the avenue's other elegant buildings—stores and churches. They gently lead the eye to the west to the more soaring buildings. At the same time, their low scale, ground-floor shopfronts, and visual amenity of landscaped rooftops reinforce the importance of Fifth Avenue as a pedestrian paradise: With protected places to sit within view of lively street life, places to shop, and places to eat, it offers a place to rest, regroup, and revive.

The British Empire Building opened in May 1933, and was the first unit constructed on Fifth Avenue. Its art displayed an imperial theme. The main entrance is surmounted by nine figures in gold leaf designed by Carl Paul Jennewein. They represent the major industries of the British Isles. Above this rests a polychromed limestone cartouche of the British coat of arms flanked by a lion and a unicorn. Across the bottom is the motto of British royalty, "Dieu et Mon Droit" (God and my right).

Above the sixth floor, recessed s

39-2

39-4

spandrel panels designed by Rene Chambellan represent the coats of arms of Wales, England, Scotland, and Ireland. The designs above the building's side entrances also relate to the British Empire's attributes.

La Maison Française opened five months later. Artist Alfred Janniot designed a bronze panel of stylized figures—representing France and New York—joining hands across the sea. Above three large figures depicting Beauté, Elegance, and Poesie stands France. She holds Notre Dame in her lap, and behind her is the motto, "Fluctuat nec Megitur" (It floats but never sinks). New York sits on a modern ocean liner in front of the 1930s skyline.

Above the door the ten-foot-high limestone cartouche of "La France" holds the torch of freedom. Rene Chambellan also designed the reliefs at the sixth floor. They depict the rise of Charlemagne's empire, the new France, Absolute Monarchy, and the

Previous pages
Fig. 39-2 A view of the excavation work for the British Empire Building and La Maison Française. At right is the steel work of the RCA Building. Courtesy: Rockefeller Center-©The Rockefeller Group, Inc.

Fig. 39-3 In 1931, Rockefeller Center construction workers receive their pay on Christmas Eve in the shadow of the Center's first Christmas tree. The lighting of the wondrous Rockefeller Center Christmas tree has become one of New York City's most endearing traditions. Courtesy: Rockefeller Center-©The Rockefeller Group, Inc.

Opposite
Fig. 39-4 The Associated Architects' marvelous International Buildings maintain Fifth Avenue's pedestrian orientation. Courtesy: Rockefeller Center-©The Rockefeller Group, Inc.

French Republic.

In 1939, the Fifth Avenue Association made its first award since 1931 to John D. Rockefeller Jr., as owner of the complex. The presentation took place at the Rockefeller Center Luncheon Club on the sixty-fifth floor of the RCA Building.

The Rockefeller Center buildings have a timeless quality, and rather than appearing old and dated, they always seem to look new and shining.

One of the Center's most beautiful stores was the Alfred Dunhill Shop in the British Empire Building. Designed by Eugene Schoen and Sons, the shop opened in 1933 (fig. 39-7). The shop epitomized masculine elegance; superb tobacco and exquisite accessories were displayed in several luxurious floors decorated in soothing shades of brown.

A 1930 guide claimed that salesmen had "Eton accents." The store was "not broadminded about other people's tobacco or lighters but [has] a large aristocratic selection of [its] own . . . To be correctly prized, everything at this shop should be viewed through a monocle."

Alfred Dunhill had been located at 514 Fifth Avenue (adjacent to Sulka) between 1923 and 1933, and moved to the elegant British Empire Building until 1990. The shop then consolidated with a branch store and moved to Park Avenue where it is again a neighbor of Sulka.

The Departure of the Vanderbilts

After trying so hard for years to battle trade, most of the Vanderbilts gave up their mansions in quick succession. Most of the seven residences that had given the avenue its aristocratic hauteur were soon reduced to dust. Sightseeing buses were forced to abandon their Fifth Avenue tour of the homes of the rich and famous.

In 1920, after the death of William D. Sloane, his widow married Henry White, the former ambassador to France. For their city residence, she kept her "Twin" house at the southwest corner of Fifty-second Street. Within a few years, however, she sold the house and moved to 854 Fifth Avenue.

The first of the Vanderbilt homes to be constructed was the last to disappear. The Southern Twin had even more than one resident because it passed through several Vanderbilt hands.

In 1920, eight years after Levi Morton left his Fifth Avenue home, his former next-door neighbor, Brigadier General Cornelius Vanderbilt III, gave up his home as well. Vanderbilt left his dwelling at 677-679 Fifth Avenue to move into the Twin house at Fifty-first Street, as a sentimental family gesture. William H. Vanderbilt, his grandfather, provided that the house would become his possession, since it had passed to his uncle George W.

39-6

Fig. 39-7 Interior view of the Alfred Dunhill store at 620 Fifth Avenue, taken in 1933, the night before the store opened. This view shows Arthur Crisp's mural, "How Britain Smokes." Photo: Rotan. Courtesy: Alfred Dunhill of London Ltd.

Previous pages
Fig. 39-5 Sculptor Lee Lawrie inspects his colossal "Atlas" as it was installed at the main entrance of the International Building in 1937. The fifteen-foot-tall bronze figure weighs fourteen thousand pounds.
Courtesy: Rockefeller Center-©The Rockefeller Group, Inc.

Fig. 39-6 This late 1930s view shows Atlas in the forecourt of the International Building. Courtesy: Rockefeller Center-©The Rockefeller Group, Inc.

Vanderbilt, who had died without leaving a son.

It was said that the Brigadier General spent $500,000 to alter the building from Victorian heaviness and gloom to eighteenth-century lightness and rococo.

Cornelius Vanderbilt III sold the mansion to William Waldorf Astor with the provision that his family be allowed to remain for one year after the closing. He died in 1942, and the southern Twin held on until 1947 when his wife moved to a mansion farther north on the avenue. The fabulous interiors were destroyed but for several magnificent items bequeathed to the Metropolitan Museum of Art. The Twin was replaced by the Crowell Publishing Company building, a nineteen-story limestone building with setbacks that was fairly sympathetic to the Rockefeller Center buildings.

(The Cammeyer shoe firm opened its De Luxe branch in a building designed by Rouse and Goldstone on the site of Vanderbilt's previous home) (extant, ground-floor alterations).

After the 1920 death of William K. Vanderbilt, his second wife, Anne Harriman Sands Rutherford, was one of the first to move to newly fashionable Sutton Place. Their French Gothic mansion on the northwest corner of Fifty-second Street was boarded up. Efforts were made to preserve it, including as the uptown office of the Empire Trust Company. But all plans fell through.

It was sold in 1925 to Benjamin Winter, who opened it to the public for charity events during its last few weeks, such as the annual benefit dance for the Dug-Out, a clubhouse and workshop for disabled ex-servicemen. Just before demolition, negotiations were opened to have the house disassembled and reassembled as a country house on Long Island. A few years later, Winter recounted that he had asked, "Can you take it down in ten days? If so, I'll do business with you. For it costs me more than $1,000 a day to hold it."[33] The dismantling project was estimated to take three years. The deal fell through and the mansion was demolished.

After announcing her move to One East Seventy-first Street, Mrs. Hamilton Twombly sold her house in 1926 at the southwest corner of Fifty-fourth Street to John D. Rockefeller, as her sister had done years earlier. He commissioned another six-story commercial building that was sympathetic to the architecture of St. Thomas Church. Revillon Frères moved into it from their building on Fifty-third Street.

William K. Vanderbilt Jr.'s mansion at 666 Fifth Avenue was demolished in the 1920s. It was ultimately replaced by a large, if undistinguished, building that extended across the entire block front. On the thirty-ninth floor of 666 Fifth Avenue, a restaurant called "Top of the Sixes" offered a superb view of the city.

William Rockefeller's East Fifty-fourth Street home which he had tried to insulate from trade, was replaced by the Aeolian Building. It had moved from Fifth Avenue and Thirty-fifth Street to 29 West Forty-second Street before moving back to the avenue. The fourteen-story building rounds the East Fifty-fourth Street corner. Of buff Indiana limestone with a pink granite base and Italian marble panels, it has delicate details like urns and garlands. Crowned by a bronze lantern, the building seems more suitable to the feminine charm of Elizabeth Arden, which moved in shortly thereafter, than to a piano recital hall.

At its 1926 annual dinner held at the Waldorf-Astoria, the Fifth Avenue Association awarded the Gould Realty Co. first prize for the Aeolian Building (selected from forty-seven new buildings constructed in the Fifth Avenue "district") and presented a certificate to architects Warren and Wetmore.

Glorious Small Shops in the Fifties

The avenue's pace had quickened from an amble to a trot. But a languid pace persisted just south of Central Park—a vestige of quieter days. The avenue's residents, fairly ancient by World War I's end, left their elegant homes for more exclusive bailiwicks. And the most elegant shops flourished. Although some exclusive shops escaped to Madison Avenue, Fifth

Fig. 41-2 Interior view of Richard Hudnut's beauty salon, ca. 1931. This mirrored delicate space contrasts with the contemporaneous "masculine" interior of the Alfred Dunhill Shop. Photo: Fay S. Lincoln. Courtesy: Historical Collections and Labor Archives, Penn State

previous page
Fig. 41-1 View of Richard Hudnut Building, ca. 1931, designed by Ely Jacques Kahn. Next door is the Aeolian Building with Elizabeth Arden's salon, which was called "deliriously lovely." Photo: Fay S. Lincoln. Courtesy: Historical Collections and Labor Archives, Penn State

Avenue remained a luxe thoroughfare. In the late 1920s the exclusive shopping district consolidated in the upper part of the avenue.

The stores which catered to deep pockets did not decline; they either disappeared or continued to their standards. In the 1920s the small shops were joined by large specialty stores, such as Saks and Bergdorf Goodman.

Since much of their tony reputations relied upon their substantial custom departments, Bergdorf, Saks, Bonwit Teller and even DePinna had garment factories over the store. The alteration department was essential. At the call, a seamstress would descend from the workshop, a fat pincushion on her wrist and a marking crayon in her pocket. After a few nips, tucks, and reassurances, she would take the garment with her. And, when the altered garment returned, it would fit absolutely perfectly. "Almost as good as custom-made," remembers a shopper fondly.

During the height of the Depression, Fifth Avenue's stores could empty any purse. While I. Miller's highest price was $20, women could purchase French handmade shoes from F. Pinet or custom-made American shoes from Bob, where shoe prices began at $50. Even flowers were costly as a guide advised people to buy their "daily gardenias" at Trepel Florists, the first on the avenue to put price tags in the window.

Precious gems continued to find the avenue a perfect setting. Between Forty-seventh and Fifty-third streets, you could buy almost priceless rubies and emeralds from Marcus and Company, or a diamond tiara from Black, Starr, & Frost. Cartier and Van Cleef & Arpels, then a block apart, were "French firms whose window displays

Fig. 42-1 This view from East Forty-ninth Street toward Fifth Avenue shows Saks Fifth Avenue under construction. Courtesy: Saks Fifth Avenue

deserve a police cordon."[28] Georg Jensen sold its silver and crafts at 667 Fifth Avenue for many years.

Also in this area were a number of the city's best beauty salons, either in their own small buildings or on the upper floors of commercial buildings. (figs. 41-1, 41-2). Women were separated into private cubicles at first. Only in more recent times have

salons become larger, open spaces for socializing and people watching. At one time, Madame Helena Rubinstein, Elizabeth Arden, and Dorothy Gray were real women with salons on the avenue. There were others, of course, like Rose Laird who offered electrified masks to "do wonders" for sagging facial muscles, or the Ogilvie Sisters, known as "henna rinse" experts.

At the southwest corner of Fifty-sixth Street, stands the beautiful Harry Winston in what looks like an impeccably restored town house. It is, however, fairly new. In 1937, the Corning Glass Works demolished a six-story building and erected in its place a building of glass block. William and Geoffrey Platt designed the building of one-inch-thick glass squares, set into a frame of Indiana limestone. The glass building was torn down when Steuben moved across the avenue.

Upper Fifth Avenue Emporiums

Saks Fifth Avenue

When Horace Saks began to assemble a site between Forty-ninth and Fiftieth streets for his new store, the move was considered almost as daring as Benjamin Altman's had been twenty years earlier. It was the first large store to move so far north. However, the National Democratic Club, at 617 Fifth Avenue, was in the middle of the proposed

Fig. 42-2 This early view of Saks Fifth Avenue emphasizes the surrounding low-scale neighborhood. A tower has been added to the rear of this designated New York City landmark, which has the virtue of being invisible from Fifth Avenue while expanding the size of Saks' selling floors. Courtesy: Saks Fifth Avenue

the store in Washington, D.C., and opened Herald Square's first department store in 1901. Saks Fifth Avenue (to differentiate it from Saks Thirty-fourth Street) was to become and remain the southern anchor of the exclusive shopping district (fig. 42-1).

The architectural firm of Starrett and Van Vleck designed a ten-story building, as an adaptation of the "later English Renaissance style." (fig. 42-2). It was Fifth Avenue's first department store to comply with the Zoning Resolution's setback requirements. With chamfered corners at Forty-ninth and Fiftieth streets, the

Fig. 42-3 Mayor Hylan at the 1924 opening of Saks Fifth Avenue on his way to lunch with Horace Saks. Courtesy: Saks Fifth Avenue

assemblage. And the club refused to sell, except for the highest price.

Allan Johnson, former CEO of Saks, tells the famous story of what happened next: Coming in by train from their New Jersey summer homes one morning, Saks and his neighbor Bernard Gimbel "were unable to sit next to each other, so they walked to the baggage car and sat on a coffin. Saks explained that he would be forced to build around the club. Gimbel stopped him and offered to speak to his Board of Directors at his Herald Square store."

His friendly competitor from Herald Square lent him over one million dollars to buy out the Democratic Club (which moved to the DeLamar Mansion at Thirty-seventh Street and Madison Avenue). And the young Adam Gimbel became Saks' assistant.

Reporters followed Saks to his home on West Eighty-sixth Street in May 1923. He announced that his real estate purchase "will assure to New York the largest store in the world specializing solely in wearing apparel and kindred lines."[29]

His father, Andrew, had founded

Fig. 42-4 A view of the third floor of Saks Fifth Avenue, ca. 1930, after the store was remodeled in the art deco style. Courtesy: Saks Fifth Avenue

building's street wall rises up to the seventh floor (which was the last of the merchandise floors) setting back at the eighth floor (offices) and ninth and tenth (stock and workrooms).

The heaviness of the rusticated granite base is offset by vast amounts of glass: Two monumental off-center entrances are flanked by enormous show windows that wrap around the entire facade. The monumental entrances are framed by carved moldings and are surmounted by cornices. The Forty-ninth Street entrance retains its original marquee.

The remarkable display windows, each framed by bronze Corinthian piers, are separated from each other by narrow strips of marble. Extending along the top of the windows is a continuous bronze grille with a delicate design; this band is surmounted by

Opposite Fig. 42-5 Sophie Gimbel, the doyenne of the Salon Moderne, adjusts a gown she had designed for actress Joan Fontaine during a photography session for a magazine. Courtesy: Saks Fifth Avenue

42-5

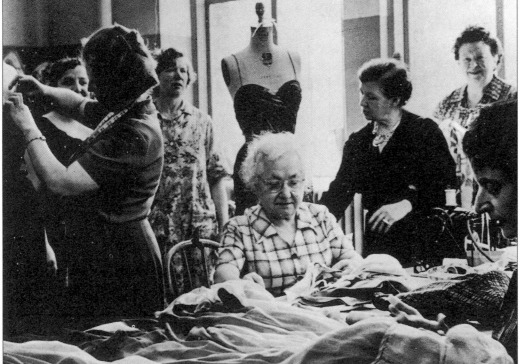

Fig. 42-6 Early view of the children's barber shop taken before the grand opening of the store. Courtesy: Saks Fifth Avenue

Fig. 42-7 A view of Mrs. Gimbel's upper-floor workroom filled with seamstresses who performed wonders with the finest fabrics. Courtesy: Saks Fifth Avenue

Fig. 42-8 A late 1930s view of Saks Fifth Avenue's shoe salon. Photo: Fay S. Lincoln. Courtesy: Historical Collections and Labor Archives, Penn State

a frieze of floral and urn motifs. Above the base, the superbly detailed facade becomes little more than a discreet background for the displayed merchandise.

When the store opened in September 1924, crowds awaited the 9:00 A.M. opening. Newspapers reported Mayor Hylan's (fig. 42-3) appearance to have lunch with Saks and that the store's first package was for President Coolidge at the White House—a silk hat in a leather hatbox.

Its windows displayed a $3,000 pigskin trunk and $1,000 raccoon coats. Uniformed doormen stood at each entrance, and an electric numbering system above the door at Fiftieth Street alerted chauffeurs parked across the street that madam had finished shopping. Yet Allan Johnson,

Fig. 42-9 A view of Saks Fifth Avenue's Christmas windows ca. 1940s. By decorating the facade as a series of Christmas trees with stars at the top and presents at the bottom, Saks brilliantly combined Christmas decorations with gift suggestions. Photo: Worsinger. Courtesy: Saks Fifth Avenue

reports that the original store initially offered "fashion at a price"—in other words, not the most expensive goods.

Its interior was much simpler than that of Lord & Taylor. *Architecture and Building* magazine noted that "the store fixtures are plainly designed in hardwood and the wall surfaces and columns are finished white above. The ceilings are flat panels in the bays with direct ceiling suspended lighting fixtures at the centers."[30]

Horace Saks died in 1926. His assistant, Adam Gimbel, a former Yale architecture student, became the store's president. He maintained the notion of a group of specialty shops within a shop. But his desire to sell luxury on a volume basis led him to revamp the store. He had the store redesigned in the luxurious art deco style and brought Antoine, the Paris hairdresser and ensconced him in a salon on the third floor (fig. 42-4). Here, clients would sit on exquisite furniture to await personal service. The Antoine de Paris beauty salon was luxurious and revolutionary—women were not separated into cubicles, but sat around, hair dripping, in one large room. But, a guide noted, "the result was worth it." In the middle of the Depression, Madame A. deBoor of the Salon deBoor was charging $300 for a series of six facials. And she had customers.

Although Saks imported many luxury goods, it also sold vast amounts of made-to-order clothing. The most famous designer was Sophie Gimbel, Adam's wife.

She designed expensive ready-to-wear, and also ruled, from the third-floor custom department, the exclusive Salon Moderne (fig. 42-5).

The workrooms on the ninth and tenth floors created all of the Salon Moderne dresses, 25 percent of the store's ready-to-wear, and 85 percent of their furs (figs. 42-6, 42-7).

Andre Perugia designed shoes for Saks that could not be released to the rest of the world for three months. After he left the store, Saks maintained the custom shoe department. A shopper says, "I used to stand on line to wait for Miss Marks, my favorite salesgirl in the shoe department" (fig. 42-8).

Saks aimed for chic in all departments. The store was credited with practically creating the costume jewelry business. Even the departments for servants' uniforms were highly regarded. All-black uniforms were encouraged for maids, but the store carried white pointed aprons, purple silk round aprons, and velour cape-coats and velvet bonnets for children's nurses. If requested, they custom made formal uniforms for chauffeurs and footmen to match car upholstery. However, the store also had the "Debutante Shop" or "Seventh Heaven" that carried good copies of haute couture.

Sidney Ring was Saks Fifth Avenue's first display director and worked at the store for thirty years. In 1927, the windows were among the first on the avenue to be designed in the art deco style which

reflected the new interior. Six windows were redesigned with silver draperies, but most of the thirty-one windows retained the mahogany paneling for the traditional room settings. At Christmastime, windows were decorated up to the third floor (fig. 42-9).

Across Forty-ninth Street, the linen store James McCutcheon moved from south of Thirty-fourth Street and opened in a narrow twelve-story building (extant, ground-floor alterations) designed by Cross and Cross in association with Starrett and Van Vleck (fig. 42-10). Their trousseaus and initialed towels and linens lasted lifetimes and even beyond.

The Tailored Woman

In 1919, Eugene K. Denton opened his specialty shop, The Tailored Woman, at 622 Fifth Avenue, at Fiftieth Street. Mr. Denton, who was born on a Tennessee plantation, started to work in retailing as a very young man in the James McCreery store on Thirty-fourth Street. In 1910, he moved to Cincinnati where he eventually opened his own store, the Denton Company.

Upon opening his first New York shop opposite the future site of Saks, Denton's advertisement declared that the goods were "carefully chosen to meet the requirements of the woman who desires well-made clothes of a simple character at fair prices." Six years later the store moved to 632 Fifth Avenue, the next block, where it remained until it had to relocate to make

Fig. 42-10 This 1957 advertisement for McCutcheon's celebrates its long tradition on the avenue. Courtesy: Seymour Durst

room for Rockefeller Center. It then moved to the southeast corner of Fifty-seventh Street; it moved in 1939 to make way for Tiffany.

For its move to 740–744 Fifth Avenue and 1 West Fifty-seventh Street in the "Bergdorf" building, it substantially enlarged its departments. The store carried conservative women's clothing; its strongest department was the fur department. Denton remembered that when he opened that store, he was surrounded by "little English shops and little French shops."

In 1968, Bergdorf Goodman bought out the remaining three years left on Denton's lease. After the deal was made, the childless Denton was quoted as saying, "I'm going to liquidate my own business without tarnishing it in any way because I don't want anyone else to have the name Tailored Woman, which I've nursed for so long."[31] Less than a year after he closed the store, the eighty-year-old Denton opened a small fur shop on Madison Avenue.

Best & Company

In 1927, the Union Club announced that it was "deserting the avenue already forsaken by the homes of many of the socially noteworthy . . . " for Park Avenue and Sixty-ninth Street. Future construction was to await the expiration of leases on some of the houses to be demolished. By moving from the home it had since 1903, the club was following its policy of "leading the advance from commercial to residential districts." After it left, the building was occupied by an art gallery.

The building was demolished for the 1947 Best & Co. twelve-story limestone building designed by Shreve, Lamb & Harmon. The-air conditioned building installed steam pipes beneath the sidewalks to melt snow and ice (fig. 42-11).

Its traditional customers—children—were well cared for. They were taken by express elevator to the children's floor. The children's barber shop had ten barbers; a baby's first haircut was 50 cents extra because a lock of hair was wrapped in cellophane for Mommy.

Philip LeBoutillier's no-nonsense attitude about clothing classics retired with him at the age of eighty-two, for he claimed to have never hired a relative. By then, the store was described as a place "for children who were seen but not heard, and for ladies who were heard but not seen. [It was] a store of superb perambulators, first haircuts, the classic look and dour warnings of Dame Fashion's sorcery . . . "[32] But Best & Co. played a role in most wealthy children's lives, and the store made money.

In 1967 the McCrory Corporation took over and the store added some fashionable departments after the former president of E. J. Korvette became president of Best & Co. The store closed within a few years and the building was demolished for Olympic Tower.

DePinna

DePinna had been located at the northwest corner of Fiftieth Street and Fifth Avenue since 1911. To make room for Rockefeller Center, the store moved to the northern Twin site in 1928. The architectural firm of Starrett and Van Vleck designed a nine-story building as an adaptation of the Florentine Renaissance style. The rusticated base held pointed arches into which were set display windows of cast and wrought bronze. The automobile entrance was on West Fifty-second Street.

The high-ceilinged ground floor had walnut counters and display cases "arranged in small sections." The walls were covered in wainscoting which extended to the height of the mezzanine at the rear. The main floor offered men's clothing, hats, and furnishings. The second floor offered boys' clothing and school outfits.

Fig. 42-11 This 1970 view shows a boys' choir from Belgium posing on Rockefeller Center's British Empire Building roof garden. The boys had a superb view of St. Patrick's Cathedral's towers and Best & Co. shortly before it was demolished to make way for Olympic Tower. Courtesy: Rockefeller Center-©The Rockefeller Group, Inc.

The third floor, with art deco decoration and furniture designed by Bouy, Inc., offered women's, misses', and girls' clothing. This was the floor where fashion took precedence over tradition. Sofas of olive and vermillion wood with orange velvet cushions and macassar ebony tables were arranged against a background of tan walls and carpets. Each dressing room was painted differently. The fourth floor sold shoes, luggage, and leather goods.

The upper floors were for office and manufacturing uses. Offices were on the fifth floor, stock and sample rooms were on the sixth floor. The cutting rooms and piece goods departments were on the seventh floor, the eighth held manufacturing and tailoring departments. The ninth floor was for the employees' dining room and rest rooms.

DePinna, which had started as a "boys' outfitter," had by this time expanded to clothing for men, women and children. In 1935, DePinna purchased the building from August Heckscher's company for $74,000 above the mortgage of $3,366,000.

The store became a favorite: "It was never ever crowded," remembers one shopper of the 1950s and 1960s (Fig. 42-12). In 1965 the building was sold to Sam Minskoff & Sons. It was reported that the store had a large number of loyal customers, but only a small percentage of them were young shoppers.

After a civilized but tearful farewell in 1969, with shoppers lined up around the block to search for bargains and their old

From middles —
to middles —
in 77 years!

In the eighties, New York's youngest gentlemen came to us for their authentic English sailor suits. The sailor suit still flourishes at De Pinna — as well as the highest in fashion for women and girls ... the finest in clothing for men and boys. Now, as then — quality is our creed, fashion our art!

De Pinna

UPPER FIFTH AVENUE at 52nd STREET, N.Y.

1036 LINCOLN ROAD, MIAMI BEACH

Fig. 42-12 DePinna had a very loyal following because it carried impeccable children's clothing as well as chic women's wear. Courtesy: Seymour Durst

salespeople, the store closed.

At the time, the vice president of the Fifth Avenue Association was quoted as saying, "We urged the owners to be selective by putting the right kind of tenant in there. It was quite a disappointment when it was rented out for political use." He was extremely upset about a banner, over one story high, with *LINDSAY* in large white letters. The building was demolished for the Pahlavi Foundation Building.

In the late 1920s, the Fifth Avenue Association's Committee of Architectural Betterment believed that commercial architecture was generally of low quality. Poorly skilled construction workers were part of the problem, but owners and builders were to be blamed because "there has been no apparent effort to produce buildings in harmony with the character of the Fifth Avenue section." The association, however, continued to grant the awards, except for 1932–1938 and during World War II, when there was virtually no construction.

The southern portion of the Colford-Jones block was demolished and replaced by the National Broadcasting Building at the northeast corner of Fifty-fifth Street (Fig. 42-13). The ground floor was occupied by stores and showrooms for Kohler; the second floor was the Chatham Phenix National Bank and Trust Company. NBC occupied sixty thousand square feet in the eleventh

through sixteenth floors, in space designed by Raymond Hood, Godley and Fouilhoux (before they designed Rockefeller Center). Offices and library spaces were on the lower floors; the upper floors included small and large recording studios, dressing rooms, and an auditorium. Mark Cross moved into a ground-floor space for a number of years (fig. 42-14).

August Heckscher demolished the two-story taxpayer on the site of the Whitney mansion. The twenty-five-story Heckscher Building rose on the spot (fig. 42-15). The limestone and white brick building, capped by a gold-colored tower, was designed by Warren and Wetmore. As originally planned, the office building was to hold a large theater, which was prohibited by law. For a short period of time, the emerging Museum of Modern Art rented exhibition space in the building.

Bonwit Teller

In 1930, Bonwit Teller moved out of its office building on Thirty-eighth Street and into its own building on the corner of East Fifty-sixth Street.

The site had been occupied by several nineteenth-century residential buildings designed by Clinton and Russell for William W. Astor. Ground floor

Opposite
Fig. 42-13 This late 1920s view of 711–715 Fifth Avenue was taken when it was the home of the National Broadcasting Company. It had been constructed on the site of the Colford-Jones row of houses. The building remains today.
Courtesy: Fifth Avenue Association

Fig. 42-14 View of Mark Cross, taken ca. 1946, when it occupied a portion of the former National Broadcasting Building. Now in Olympic Tower, Mark Cross has moved up the avenue since the early days of the century. Photo: Fay S. Lincoln. Courtesy: Historical Collections and Labor Archives, Penn State

Opposite
Fig.42-15 Early view of the Heckscher Building, now the Crown Building, shortly after its erection on the southwest corner of Fifty-seventh Street. The gilded statues have not yet been installed over the Fifth Avenue entrance. The Huntington mansion, guarded by small lions, is in the foreground. Courtesy: Cushman & Wakefield

commercial uses were installed after 1910, including the famous Elysée Restaurant. The buildings were demolished to make way for the new store of Stewart & Company, which had moved from Thirty-seventh Street. The firm again hired Warren and Wetmore to design its building.

In 1929, while construction was underway, Stewart and Company moved to temporary quarters on Fiftieth Street and Fifth Avenue, a costly mistake that may have been lethal.

Opening a few days before the 1929 Stock Market crash, the twelve-story

Fig. 42-16 Ely Jacques Kahn's simplified facade for Bonwit Teller, ca. 1938. The building was demolished for Trump Tower. Tiffany & Co. had not yet been built next door. Courtesy: Municipal Archives, Department of Records & Information Services, City of New York

building's dedication was a major public event. The severe limestone facade was Fifth Avenue's first example of absolutely modern architecture—the art deco style.

The building's focal point was its oversized ornamented entrance. Above the second floor was the gigantic lettering of STEWART and Company, set like a lintel over posts separating the central doorways from two flanking display windows. Above the doorways was a large faience tile and glass panel of a woman looking at herself in the mirror flanked by two smaller panels.[34]

The store foundered and Bonwit Teller signed a long-term lease for the building.

By the following July, Ely Jacques Kahn had begun renovating the new building for Bonwit Teller, which moved into it in September 1930 (fig. 42-16). The entrance and interiors were simplified. The more subdued result was appropriate for the Depression and for the conservative store that Bonwit Teller was at the time. Retaining many of the luxurious interior finishes, Kahn obliterated many of the small shops and alcoves so that the spaces were grander.

Bonwit Teller evolved into an extremely chic women's specialty store with clothing that ranged from moderately priced to very expensive. The Safari Room sold contemporary, very expensive and exclusive designs. Yet the store also had a temporary shop called the Finale Shop which sold marked-down clothing for two months at the end of the spring and fall seasons.

Sarah Tomerlin Lee remembers that in the 1930s some important papers flew out of an executive's window onto the avenue. "There was not a scrap of paper on the avenue in those days," she said. After digging around the trash, she asked the young uniformed boy at the front door to check the trash cans down the avenue. He came back in twenty minutes, with creased papers rescued from an assortment of receptacles. She rewarded him with five dollars. "Oh, no," said the youngster, whose job it was to help shoppers with packages, and dog waterings, "I couldn't take that. This is my job and I'm proud to work for Bonwit Teller." And most employees felt the same way.

With a gleam in her eye, a woman who worked in the advertising department in the 1960s says, "I loved Bonwit Teller's 721 Club. It was an evening Christmas shopping club for men. We'd serve champagne, models would wander around in 'at-home wear,' as we called it . . . And we would help the guys pick out gifts for their wives or mistresses. We had to be very adept and discreet, of course."

Bonwit Teller became part of Genesco, Inc., a Nashville company, as a result of two acquisitions in 1956 and 1965. The *New York Times* reported that in its last years one of the leading carriage trade stores "and later a contemporary fashion leader in New York and the East was a victim of inconsistency in both management and policy by Genesco . . ."[35]

The Bonwit Teller building came to a bizarre end. The building was planned to be demolished for the young Donald Trump's Trump Tower. He was able to increase the proposed building's height by using the unused development rights above the adjacent Tiffany Building. Preservationists' fears about the loss of the art deco architecture were somewhat allayed, however, because various stone and metal ornaments were to be saved. Stone figures of partially draped nudes between the eighth and ninth floors had been "sought with enthusiasm by the Metropolitan Museum." A gallery owner was quoted as saying, "The reliefs are as important as the sculpture on [the] Rockefeller [Center] buildings." However, construction workers demolished them. An official of the Trump Organization was reported to say, "the merit of these stones was not great enough to justify the effort to save them . . ."[36]

On the other hand, people thought that the grillwork above the entrance was successfully removed. Created of Benedict nickel, the grilles were of particularly heavy metal and required polishing. Once removed, they soon disappeared. Otto Teegen, commissioned by Ely Jacques Kahn to design the metalwork fifty years earlier, was interviewed after the disappearance. He told the newspaper, "It's odd that a person like Trump, who is spending $100 million on this building, should squirm that it might cost as much as $32,000 to take down those panels."

Bergdorf Goodman

In 1925, Mrs. Alice G. Vanderbilt, the widow of Cornelius Vanderbilt, filed a petition in Supreme Court to sell their thirty-five-year-old chateau for $7 million in cash. After her husband's death in 1899, his will provided for her life use of the property. His will also provided that upon her death, the property was to go to his sons Alfred Gwynne (who had since died on the *Lusitania*) or Reginald. Son Cornelius III had been left out of the will because the elder Vanderbilt disapproved of his 1896 marriage to a southerner, Grace Wilson. The property could be sold only when his children's generation had expired, with the proceeds divided among his daughters' children. Therefore, all Vanderbilt heirs (children, grandchildren, and great-grandchildren) were required to join in the legal approval of the sale.

Claiming that holding on to the property was a financial burden, Mrs. Vanderbilt said that her taxes had increased 400 per cent, from $38,446 to $129,120, since she had taken possession of the home. Asserting that her home was no longer an appropriate residential site, her court papers cited the commercial nature of the neighborhood, with the Heckscher Building and the recent sale of the Collis Huntington home at the southeast corner of Fifty-seventh Street. She also claimed that it would be difficult and prohibitively expensive to convert the adaptation of the Chateau de Blois to commercial use.

Fig. 42-17 View of architects Buchman & Kahn's Bergdorf Goodman building. At that time, Bergdorf occupied several portions of the building, with The Tailored Woman, Van Cleef & Arpels, and Delman Shoes as fellow tenants. Courtesy: Bergdorf Goodman

Fig. 42-18 View of the "fab" Bigi boutique, ca. late 1960s, designed by Tom Lee. The clothing and design of this department—young, light, fun—was a departure from the rest of the store. Courtesy: Collection of Sarah Tomerlin Lee

During World War I, she had allowed the Red Cross to fill the ballroom with sewing machines to make garments for soldiers.

Permission to sell was granted, and she moved to East Sixty-seventh Street. Negotiations were underway to move the home to Sands Point to be used for the home

of the Harbor Hills Country Club, on the site of the 125-acre estate of Julius Fleischmann. A few things were salvaged, such as a marble fireplace with caryatids supporting the mantle, designed by Augustus Saint-Gaudens (now in the Metropolitan Museum), and the front gate

(now at Central Park and 105th Street). Marcus Loew salvaged the mosaics from the Moorish smoking room for the womens' lounge in the Midland Theater in Kansas City.

Despite plans for a forty-two-story hotel on the site, the chateau was ultimately

Fig. 42-19 This is a view of a portion of the "B and G" shop, which offered complete wardrobes for children from birth to childhood. The shop was redesigned in the 1960s by Tom Lee. Photo: Henry S. Fullerton. Courtesy: Collection of Sarah Tomerlin Lee

replaced by Bergdorf Goodman. Almost a purlieu of Paris, the store has remained the avenue's most exclusive and European store.

In 1928, Buchman & Kahn designed a marble building like no other on the avenue (fig. 42-17). Compared to the robust commercial palazzi, this delicate building was designed to appeal to refined female clients. The facade of white South Dover marble, with green bronzed-trimmed windows, balcony, and doorways, and green tile roof, appeared to be a row of elegant town houses. Beneath the unified facade Bergdorf Goodman shared the structure with other exclusive shops.

The Bergdorf Goodman interiors were French, with Rococo, Empire, and art deco ornamentation. While creating a luxurious background, the small, impeccably detailed spaces reassured Edwin Goodman that if the store didn't succeed, the rooms could be rented to other tenants.

The main entrance on West Fifty-eighth Street led to an elliptical rotunda which separated the Fifth Avenue room for womens' accessories from the rear room for millinery. Little merchandise was displayed throughout the store. After a customer made a request, a model would be summoned to display the clothing. With its intimate spaces and titled European employees, the store had a very European ambiance, more so than any of the other Fifth Avenue stores.

Until the end of World War I, rich women had most of their "important dresses" made to order, a time-consuming process. Although Americans had full pocketbooks, they had little time for the repeated visits required for custom-made clothing. Bergdorf Goodman became the first of the custom houses to sell these dresses ready to wear, at custom prices.

The store reflected Edwin Goodman's credo that the store should offer superb quality and the most attentive service. Leonard Hankin, retired executive vice president of Bergdorf Goodman, began to work in the store during the Depression. He remembered that Edwin Goodman took personal interest in each employee—"he even told me where to buy a suit and get my hair cut." At the time, the store had major custom departments for millinery, clothing, and furs. Accessories, such as minaudières and beaded handbags, and the finest perfumes from Europe, were few and well chosen.

Even during the Depression, the store did well because it catered to society's richest women. In fact, the building was foreclosed and was taken over by an insurance company; Goodman purchased it for approximately $3,600,000, subject to a mortgage of $2,750,000.

Seven floors above Fifth Avenue was a large garment factory with thousands of padded forms, seamstresses, and bolts of fabric. The "silk room" held the finest fabrics; there were separate rooms for the creation of coats, blouses, suits, dresses, hats, and furs. Above it all was the twenty-room penthouse of Edwin Goodman and his wife, living as "janitor" and "janitress" as required by the city's codes.

Mr. Hankin remembers that the millinery department was very important because women always wore hats. "Women used to come in for hours at a time and chat and gossip, the way people today talk to hairdressers and psychiatrists." Before he became a clothing designer, Halston was the store's exclusive milliner.

While continuing to cultivate the store's European flavor, Edwin Goodman, who preferred the custom departments, entrusted his ready-to-wear to three young Americans under the age of twenty-five: his daughter Ann; his son, Andrew, who had worked for a short time in Paris for designer Jean Patou; and Bernard Newman, a former window dresser at Russeks, who became a clothing designer.

Mr. Hankin remembers suggesting in a lengthy memo to Edwin Goodman that a "Miss Bergdorf" department for young women be started. A week of silence followed. Then, he was invited to an elegant lunch "in the apartment." He, Edwin, and Andrew spoke of everything but business. Over cigars and brandy, Edwin told him, "I agree with everything you said. And you and Andrew can do it after I'm dead." Edwin Goodman died in 1953, and Andrew, known as Mr. Andrew, took over. The Miss Bergdorf department opened shortly after Edwin's death and the Bigi department opened in the mid 1960s (figs. 42-18, 42-19).

In 1914, Edwin Goodman had hired Ethel Frankau, who became the doyenne of the store's custom salon. He had offered her a job after he saw a dress she had designed, worn by her older sister, scenic designer Aline Bernstein. Frankau stayed at the store for more than fifty years, until she was replaced in the 1960s by Elieth Roux, a young Frenchwoman who had been directrice of Christian Dior in Paris.

Mme. Roux, a woman who epitomizes international chic and class, remembers feeling that the ambiance at Bergdorf was like that of a European salon. The couture department was on the second floor facing the Plaza and Andrew Goodman would stop by to chat with his favorite customers.

To assemble collections, she traveled to Europe for weeks at a time. She would return with one model of each design along with sufficient materials, thread, buttons, and whatever else was necessary to

create as many garments as she thought would be sold. After a customer ordered the model, the seamstresses from the seventh floor ateliers recreated it centimeter by centimeter. Price was not an important factor. The custom departments were gradually phased out in the late 1970s, although the custom fur department lasted longer, with certain exclusive lines created only for Bergdorf's.

There were never crowds at Bergdorf's—even on the main floor which was occupied mostly by Hermes on one side and Delman shoes on the other. Delman, a leased department, had its own entrance on Fifth Avenue. Mme. Roux said, "You never knew who you would bump into at Delman's," a chandelier-lit space staffed by men.

Mr. Hankin remembers that after The Tailored Woman left the building, the ground-floor space was reorganized and the store expanded. Van Cleef & Arpels moved into the Fifty-seventh Street corner. Delman shoes were sent upstairs and the ground floor became more compartmentalized.

It remains a beautiful space, with luxurious finishes, exquisite cases, and helpful salespeople. Yet it doesn't seem like the private but welcoming women's club it was in the past.

Opposite
Fig. 42-20 A ca. 1938 view of 745 Fifth Avenue, known as the Squibb Building and the home of FAO Schwarz for many years. The Savoy-Plaza Hotel is to the left. Photo: Fay S. Lincoln. Courtesy: Historical Collections and Labor Archives, Penn State

After Bergdorf Goodman was constructed, Mrs. Mary Mason Jones's home, a reminder of the nineteenth century, stood for a while. The piece of Marble Row had been minimally altered for use as a branch office of the New York Trust Company. It looked much as it had when Mrs. Jones, later Mrs. Paran Stevens, and even later, Mrs. Hermann Oelrichs lived in it.

At the Fifty-eighth Street corner, the Mason houses were demolished for the thirty-two-story 745 Fifth Avenue, built by Abe Adelson in 1931 and designed by Ely Jacques Kahn (fig. 42-20). The stark art deco building was known to generations of children for the toy store, FAO Schwarz, which moved into the building in the early 1930s. The toy store had opened in New York on Broadway opposite A. T. Stewart with this motto: "To offer the best goods, at most reasonable prices, with polite attention."

Tiffany & Company

Earlier in the century, Tiffany & Co. had been one of the first stores to move to the avenue north of Thirty-fourth Street. It remained at the corner of East Thirty-seventh Street long after the other jewelers had gone. Within reach of dime stores and inexpensive women's clothing shops, the store finally added a nameplate above its Fifth Avenue entrance in 1935. But it never lost its ambiance. A 1930 guide noted, "The heads of the precious stone department are steeped in the lore of old jewels, and as a result their settings give an air of glamour to even the lowly zircon."[37]

It moved to the southeast corner of Fifty-seventh Street on a site previously occupied by Park & Tilford, James Robinson, Inc., and The Tailored Woman. The architectural firm of Cross and Cross designed the eight-story Tiffany Building, which was awarded the Fifth Avenue Association's gold medal for its 1940 architectural competition (fig. 42-21). Douglas L. Elliman, chairman of the Association's Committee on Architectural Awards, explained that Tiffany was "a modern structure adapted to the tempo of present-day merchandising methods and represents a worthy architectural contribution to the notable group of buildings erected in recent years in the vicinity of Fifth Avenue and Fifty-seventh Street."[38]

The facade is limestone over a two-story base of granite. The severe design is softened by the use of pinkish marble framing the windows. Atlas and his clock guards the entrance.

Trusses supporting the second floor made first floor columns unnecessary; the first floor salesroom is a grand, air-conditioned space (fig. 42-22). The selling rooms are minimally ornamented, but constructed of the most beautiful materials. The teak and burled walnut display cases rest on marble bases; some of the teak-lined walls contain inset display cases.

With highly polished surfaces and the absence of ornamentation, the store has an ambiance at once timeless, classic and

Fig. 42-22 This contemporary view of Tiffany's main floor shows how well timeless luxury has aged—little has changed in fifty years, and it is as beautiful as ever.
Courtesy: Tiffany & Co.

Opposite
Fig. 42-21 Tiffany & Co.'s current store at Fifth Avenue and Fifty-seventh Street. Atlas, supporting his
clock, guards this front door, as he has guarded the store's entrances since the nineteenth century.
Courtesy: Tiffany & Co.

modern. When it opened, the main floor offered precious and semiprecious jewelry, pearls, and watches. The mezzanine had private salesrooms and stationery; the second floor sold silverware, clocks, and leather goods; the third floor displayed china and glass. Silver polishing, jewelry design, and watch repair were on the upper floors.

In 1955, Walter Hoving, president of the Hoving Corporation (which owned Bonwit Teller) took over the store. In a move to bring the store into the twentieth century and yet restore its nineteenth-century reputation, he held the store's first storewide sale to get rid of anything less than exquisite, such as leather and silverplate. He brought Gene Moore, Bonwit Teller's display designer, to create his beautiful windows and Jean Schlumberger from his own shop to design fantastic jewelry. Although the store again offers leather goods and scarves, they are very expensive and could never be considered anything but the best.

Fifth Avenue at Night

Although the city boasted more modern hotels and newer night spots, in the 1930s, Fifth Avenue's hotels had maintained their charm. In the midst of all of the destruction and resurrection, they remained, grand, expensive and glamorous. The Waldorf had muddled through its last days like a sick whale. These smaller, more elegant, more sylphlike hotels changed their public rooms to suit fashion, but never their attitude. There was something very modern about these old-fashioned hotels. The public spaces were fairly compact and their bars and lounges were easier to convert to restaurants than gigantic rooms.

The St. Regis Hotel

The St. Regis Hotel, still deluxe, was

Fig. 43-1 The Iridium Room, where black tie attire was de rigueur. Courtesy: St. Regis Hotel

expanded down East Fifty-fifth Street in 1927. In 1938, the Iridium Room, considered by some to be the best (and most expensive) place to dance in the city, opened in the basement. The dance floor slid back to reveal an ice skating rink for professional skaters to entertain during breaks in the dancing (fig. 43-1). A guide mused, "The women waltz like blown wisps of silk, their feet barely touching the floor, when Charles Brown and his orchestra play the 'Blue Danube,' which they do at least once every evening. There is a low buzz of well-bred conversation. Waiters in full-dress uniform flutter to and fro with silver-topped dishes."[39]

The Viennese Roof opened after two floors were added to the top of the building. Its name was changed to the more neutral-sounding St. Regis Roof, in the naive words of 1939, "because of fear of the popular bitterness toward Germany."[40] The roof, decorated in pink, remained a choice location for debutante balls, weddings, and charity events. But it was one of the city's most beautiful places in which to dance in nice weather. The food continued to be divine and costly; people used to step out on the penthouse terrace for cocktails.

In those days, one of New York's greatest society figures, Prince Serge Obolensky, served as "Vincent Astor's unofficial master of ceremonies" (fig. 43-2). One of his ideas was the Maisonette Russe, which became the St. Regis Maisonette.

The hotel's night spots—whether

Fig.43-2 Prince Serge Obolensky at the St. Regis Roof. Courtesy: St. Regis Hotel

Fig. 43-3 The Old King Cole mural was painted by American artist Maxfield Parrish in 1906 for the Knickerbocker Hotel on West Forty-second Street. It was hung in the St. Regis's King Cole Grill in 1932, and was recently rehung in the new King Cole Bar. Courtesy: St. Regis Hotel

Fig. 43-4 Contemporary view of the guest lobby of the recently renovated St. Regis Hotel. Courtesy: St. Regis Hotel

Fig. 43-5 The Plaza Hotel's fabulous Persian Room, ca. 1934. Photo: Fay S. Lincoln. Courtesy: Historical Collections and Labor Archives, Penn State

the intimate La Boîte or the larger and elegant Maisonette—never lost their luster, even into the 1960s. Reflecting the lives of their tony patrons who summered elsewhere, the rooms were closed during June, July, and August.

A large mural of Old King Cole by Maxfield Parrish was removed from Astor's former Knickerbocker Hotel on West Forty-second Street (fig. 43-3). It was installed in 1932, in the King Cole grill, a clubby space—for men that is. Women were permitted to enter after 4:00 P.M. When the grill was transformed into the Lespinasse restaurant, the mural was moved into the new bar.

The hotel, which remained a society favorite, had changed little through the years (fig. 43-4). It underwent a $100 million renovation and reopened in 1991 with all of its former glory restored, and maybe a bit more.

Plaza Hotel

Tea at the Plaza Hotel in the main lounge was served by waiters in livery for 80 cents and taken by people who never "heard of strikes, depressions or revolutions . . ."41

The Plaza Hotel's Persian Room opened in the hotel's former Rose Room. The restaurant, featuring Lillian Gaertner Palmedo's large murals based on Persian miniatures, was the only place in New York where Eddy Duchin and his orchestra performed for public dancing (fig. 43-5).

Fig. 43-6 A sophisticated evening in the Rainbow Room, ca. late 1930s. The Rainbow Room has recently been restored to its previous splendor. Courtesy: Rockefeller Center-©The Rockefeller Group, Inc.

Behind velvet draperies, Helen Worden wrote in *Here is New York*: "Cigarette smoke, heavy perfumes, the fragrance of bruised gardenias and the odor of appetizing foods touch your nostrils. Beautiful, bejewelled women drift in . . . a waiter beckons. You follow him into the soft black room with its firefly lights. You are vaguely aware of faces, white shirt fronts, bare shoulders and small tables. The waiter jerks back two chairs. You and your escort slip in . . . "

Rainbow Room

Not as expensive, but with a breathtaking view, was the Rainbow Room, sixty-five floors above Rockefeller Center (fig. 43-6). For $3.50 (in 1939) dinner was served to music by "Alec Templeton, the blind pianist," and Al Donahue's dance orchestra. The dance floor of the quintessential nightclub was encircled by bronze railings that were supported by lighted crystal balls. The recent renovation and culinary overhaul of the Rainbow Room has made it once again one of the city's most beautiful restaurants. For far more than $3.50, people dine and feel transported back into a more glamorous and graceful era.

Savoy-Plaza Hotel

The white Savoy-Plaza was completed in 1930. Called New York's "international country club," the thirty-three story hotel, designed by McKim, Meade & White, was the final piece of the Grand Army Plaza— white buildings with green roofs edging the open space. The avenue's newest hotel had the shortest life.

The avenue's hotels aged gracefully. When fashion moved east to Park Avenue, they held on. When fashion demolished many of the Park Avenue beauties, the Fifth Avenue hotels were still there. And that has always been part of their charm and allure. What past generations considered terribly modern, now offers comfort amid a sense of history. Even the Gotham Hotel, which deteriorated and went through a series of incarnations, has reemerged. As the Peninsula, it is a miracle of art nouveau.

When the Savoy-Plaza was demolished for the General Motors building, New Yorkers mourned the loss of the hotel and its fabulous shops. "Who needs a plaza on Fifth Avenue?" they asked. Others were affronted that on the city's grandest pedestrian boulevard a building was going to feature an automobile showroom. But recently, FAO Schwarz, the toy store, has moved into the white building). And there is no happier use for the plaza than to be overrun with sated children and exhausted parents.

So, sometimes there are good endings from sad demolitions of favored buildings. But the old buildings are the ones that hold our hearts and our memories. And in the last few years, all of the hotels have undergone superb renovations, reinforcing the importance of Fifth Avenue. These now serve as reminders of the best of the avenue's past, while also reminding us that the past can live on, in fact, if we cherish it.

1. *New York Times*, September 16, 1928.

2. *Highlights of Manhattan*, p. 64.

3. *The New Yorker*, September 9, 1939.

4. Leonard S. Marcus, *The American Store Window*, p. 30.

5. Ibid.

6. James C. Young, "Fifth Avenue's Changing Tide," *New York Times*, July 17, 1927.

7. *New York Times*, July 26, 1927.

8. *New York Times*, February 13, 1929.

9. Gretta Palmer, *A Shopping Guide to New York*, page 78.

10. *Women's Wear Daily*, April 11, 1962.

11. *New York Times*, April 8, 1928.

12. *The New Yorker*, November 20, 1937.

13. *New York Times*, October 5, 1934.

14. Gretta Palmer, *A Shopping Guide to New York*, page 15.

15. "French Art Moderne Exposition in New York," *Good Furniture*, March 1928, p. 119.

16. Elizabeth Cory, *New York Times*, March 4, 1928.

17. *New York Times*, February 19, 1928.

18. "Building for S. H. Kress and Company," *Architectural Forum*, February 1936, p. 90.

19. Walter R. Brooks, *New York:An Intimate Guide*, p. 201.

20. Nathan Silver, *Lost New York*, p. 65.

21. Jonathan Goldman, *Empire State Building Book*.

22. *New York Times*, December 14, 1930.

23. *New York Times*, February 21, 1926.

24. Tom Schachtman, *Skyscraper Dreams: The Great Real Estate Dynasties of New York*, p. 126.

25. F. S. Laurence, "On the Passing of Delmonico's. An Architectural Landmark," *Architecture*, November 1925, p. 420.

26. *New York Times*, November 6, 1927.

27. Geoffrey Moorehouse, *Imperial City*, p. 19.

28. Walter R. Brooks, *New York: An Intimate Guide*, p. 188.

29. *New York Times*, May 4, 1923.

30. "Saks New Department Store, *Architecture and Building*, October 1924, p. 156.

31. *New York Times*, November 13, 1967.

32. *Women's Wear Daily*, April 11, 1962.

33. *New York Times*, September 16, 1928.

34. Christopher Gray, *The Bonwit Teller Building* (report).

35. *New York Times*, January 26, 1979.

36. *New York Times*, June 6, 1980.

37. Gretta Palmer, *A Shopping Guide to New York*, p. 101.

38. *New York Times*, March 30, 1941.

39. Helen Worden, *Here Is New York*, p. 93.

40. Ibid.

41. Helen Worden, *Here Is New York*, p. 131.

Avenue of Memories

"C'est magnifique!" says a Parisian friend about a spring walk along Fifth Avenue. "We have nothing so new, so bright in Europe." Yet Americans complain that little remains of the route's lustre. Yes, it has changed; many blocks have been altered beyond recognition. The avenue is transforming, again. And the worst is over, I think.

With grand hotels, tall buildings, and expensive stores as both its scenery and stage, Fifth Avenue remains a thoroughfare of memories, wishes, and desires. So we mourn each change. A treasured store

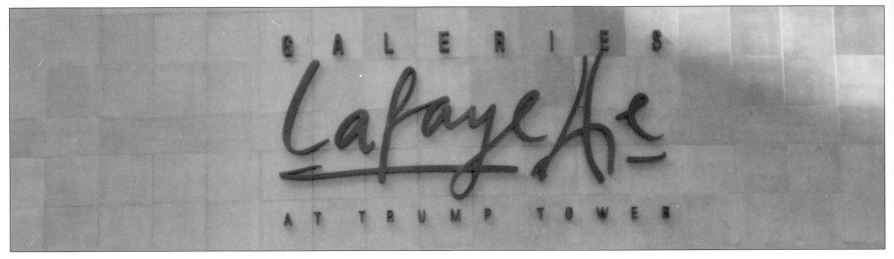

closes, a building we admired is demolished. We can feel young so long as our favorite salesclerk is old. When we bemoan the avenue's transitions, perhaps we confront our feelings of mortality and aging. The avenue is crammed with memories, but the clues that trigger the reminiscences have disappeared. We can never show out-of-town pals where we got our first haircut or bought our first minidress. A walk up the avenue becomes an effort of trying to bring back the memories.

Occasionally, I carry an old shopping bag decorated by Bonwit Teller's signature spray of flowers or B. Altman's oxblood-colored monogram. Women glance over. Then, they look a second time. And they smile tightly, almost grimace as if to acknowledge a fellow member of a secret club.

However, I was almost relieved when Trump Tower's Bonwit Teller disappeared. The narrow vertical space had little to do with the "real" Bonwit's of chicly exotic clothing and attentive salesclerks. Its

replacement—Galeries Lafayette—seems perfect. With its European ambiance and French accented clerks, the store is a larger version of the many little French shops that decorated the avenue fifty years ago.

Unlike other avenues that may be particularly wide or beautifully landscaped, Fifth Avenue's classic elegance depends on two things: its buildings and its pedestrians. Each of the avenue's designated New York City landmarks helps to reinforce this grace. The New York Public Library, the Cartier building, the Knox building, the street clock at Forty-third Street, and the Fred F. French building seem to mock the new structures as overdressed parvenus. Others, like the former Tiffany building or the lone Marble Twin, stand as ravaged beauties.

The perfection of the Frick Museum or the Morgan Library makes me wonder about the vanished possibilities of a museum in one of the Vanderbilt homes. Instead, the avenue offers me the luxuries of the cool, slightly scented air when I have tea in the St. Regis or a cocktail in the Peninsula, or a peek at the Plaza's Eloise. Sitting on the library's landscaped terrace or walking through the dim splendor of Cartier are among the city's eternal pleasures. Jewels at Harry Winston or Cartier or a minaudière from Tiffany may be out of my reach, but it comforts me that my city has these wonders for sale.

For years, people predicted the demise of the avenue. They blamed suburban malls, leveraged buyouts, discount stores, everything or anything. "After all," a friend said, "we can't expect a 'Fifth Avenue address' to mean much if the shopping that made it famous disappears." In the 1980s the newest tidal wave began to overtake the avenue. Specialty stores closed, bookstores disappeared, limestone was pulverized. With office towers proposed, the avenue was on its way to becoming a nice street on which to *work*.

Just recently, a few helping hands came to save the avenue from near-drowning. Some of the lifesavers go by the names of Henri Bendel, St. John, Lord & Taylor, Saks Fifth Avenue, Christian Dior, and Kenneth Jay Lane.

Fifth Avenue is not in decline; it continues to reinvent itself. After renovations, with millions of dollars literally washing soot and age away, the avenue's hotels older hotels now outshine their younger rivals. Lord & Taylor and Saks Fifth Avenue have been meticulously

enlarged. Henri Bendel's renovation has provided the perfect setting for the precious Lalique windows. Water again flows from the Pulitzer Fountain. Streets are kept clean

by industrious workers dressed in white and hired by property owners' taxes. New Yorkers bask in the beauty and tranquility of the gloriously renovated library and Bryant Park. The cacophonous Trump Tower is filled with expensive and international shops. Tourists ask the timeless questions, but their accents are from Japan or Germany, not Indiana. And Doubleday, Brentano's/Scribner's, Ferragamo, Bulgari, Gucci, Buccelatti, Fortunoff's, Mark Cross, Charles Jourdan, and Steuben Glass are like permanent guests on the avenue.

With many shops located in older buildings, the tradition of gleaming show windows cut into limestone facades is wonderfully preserved. Some people adore the new, thin skinned buildings with their marble-lined atria. I don't. I think that a posh store deserves a limestone frame. Masonry bases with deep-set windows continue the avenue's formality and pedestrian orientation. And one of the most welcome additions to Fifth Avenue is the Nat Sherman store. With bronze Indians flanking its clock perched on the corner of Salmon Tower, the shop reinvents a corner that hasn't had an interesting store in years. "Forty-second Street and Fifth Avenue is the greatest corner in the

world for a real New York store," says Joel Sherman, echoing Walter Salmon's sentiment of sixty years earlier.

There are few grander sights imaginable than the B. Altman building glowing again. Everyone is looking forward to its reincarnation as the New York Resource Center. But there are many other important revivals along the avenue: the restoration of the Empire State Building's original dull-red window frames, the Fred F. French Building's startling polychromy, and the rejuvenation of 745 Fifth Avenue as the home of Bergdorf Goodman's Men's Store. And small buildings like the renovated former McCutcheon and Hardman Piano

buildings also help maintain the shoppers' sense of scale.

Even the street vendors know that the avenue is special: One hose seller hung up a sign on his table that proclaimed, "Socks Fifth Avenue." Fake Rolex watches are sold in front of the Rolex Building and pseudo Gucci T-shirts are displayed near the Gucci shop. It's almost amusing. But the issue of street vendors has not been resolved in eighty years. And it's become a harder question to answer. The Fifth Avenue Association continues its task, along with other civic and governmental groups, looking for ways to preserve the elegance and, frankly, elitism of the street, while

supporting people's personal rights.

At the 1991 opening of "Coca-Cola Fifth Avenue" in the building that formerly housed Mark Cross, visitors had a grand time searching for souvenirs. Yet, amid the fun, a fashion coordinator from Saks Fifth Avenue was quoted as sighing and saying, "The start of the decline of Fifth Avenue. Coke doesn't go with Fendi, if you know what I mean." To some it sounded like a complaint. To me, it was reassuring. After a hundred years we're still lamenting the deterioration of the avenue. That means that we still think it's special enough to preserve.

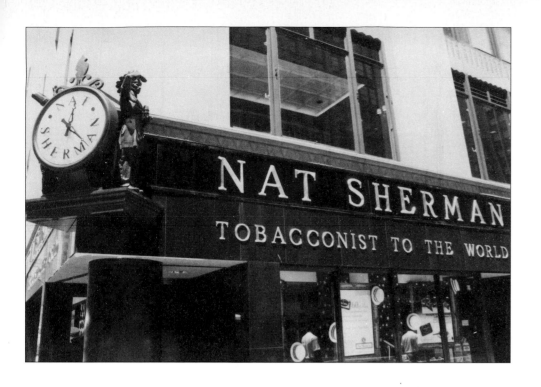

BIBLIOGRAPHY

Alpern, Andrew, and Seymour Durst. *HOLDOUTS!* New York: McGraw-Hill Book Co., 1984.

B. Altman & Co. *B. Altman & Company's Enlarged Store*: New York, 1914.

Benson, Susan Porter. *Counter Cultures: Saleswomen, Managers, and Customers in American Department Stores 1890–1940*. Urbana: University of Illinois Press, 1986.

Bottomley, William Lawrence. "The Architecture of Retail Stores," *Architectural Forum*. June 1924.

Brock, H. I., and J. W. Golinkin. *New York Is Like This*. New York: Dodd, Mead, 1929.

Brooks, Walter R. *New York: An Intimate Guide*. New York: Alfred A. Knopf, 1931.

Brown, Henry Collins. *Fifth Avenue Old and New, 1824–1924*. New York, 1924.

"Building Erected by Stewart & Co. Altered for Bonwit Teller." *American Architect*. November 1930.

Chase, W. Parker. *New York, The Wonder City*. New York: Wonder City Publishing Co., 1932.

Collins, J. F. L.. *Both Sides of Fifth Avenue*. New York: J. F. L. Collins, 1910.

Consumers League of New York. *Do Your Best to Conserve Our National Resources in Man and Woman Power*. New York, 1917.

David, A. C. "The New Fifth Avenue," *Architectural Record*. July 1907.

1866 Guide to New York City. Reprint: New York: Schocken Books, 1975.

Embury, Aymar II. "From Twenty-third Street Up—Part Two," *The Brickbuilder*. November 1916.

Ferry, John William. *A History of the Department Store*. New York: Macmillan Co., 1960.

Fifth Avenue Association. *Fifty Years on Fifth 1907–1957*. New York: Fifth Avenue Association, 1957.

Fifth Avenue Bank of New York. *Fifth Avenue Events*. New York: Fifth Avenue Bank, 1916.

Fifth Avenue From Start to Finish. New York: Welles & Co., 1911.

Foreman, John, and Robbe Pierce Stimson. *The Vanderbilts and the Gilded Age*. New York: St. Martins' Press, 1991.

Gillon, Edmund Vincent. *Beaux-Arts Architecture in New York: A Photographic Guide*. New York: Dover Publications, 1988.

Goldman, Jonathan. *The Empire State Building Book*. New York: St. Martin's Press, 1980.

Good Furniture. "French Art Moderne Exposition in New York." March 1928.

Gray, Christopher. *The Bonwit Teller Building*. Report prepared for Bonwit Teller, Inc., 1978.

Haddon, Rawson, W. "Some Recent Salesroom Interiors," *Architecture*. July 1917.

Hart, Harold H. *Hart's Guide to New York City*. New York: Hart Publishing Co., 1964.

Hastings, Charles Warren. "The Lord & Taylor Building," *Architecture and Building*. March 1914.

Herndon, Booton. *Bergdorf's on the Plaza: The Story of Bergdorf Goodman*. New York: Alfred A. Knopf, 1956.

Hillis, Marjorie. *New York, Fair or No Fair: A Guide for the Woman Vacationist*. New York: The Bobbs-Merrill Company, 1939.

Hendrickson, Robert. *The Grand Emporiums*. Briarcliff Manor, New York: Scarborough Books, 1980.

Hooper, Parker Morse. "Ornamental Shop Fronts," *The Architectural Forum*. June 1924.

Hoskins, Robert. "Lord & Taylor—The Signature of American Style," *Visual Merchandising and Store Design*. April 1991.

Hudnut, Joseph. "Tiffany & Co.," *Architectural Forum*. June 1941.

Irwin, Will. *Highlights of Manhattan,*. rev. ed., New York: D. Appleton Century Co., 1937.

James, Theodore. *Fifth Avenue*. New York: Walker, 1971.

King, Moses. *King's Handbook of New York City. 1893*, reprint, New York: Benjamin Blom, 1972.

King, Robert B., and Charles O. McLean. *The Vanderbilt Homes*. New York: Rizzoli, 1989.

Klein, Alexander, ed. *The Empire City: A Treasury of New York*. New York: Rinehart & Co., 1955.

Laurence, F. S. "On the Passing of Delmonico's, An Architectural Landmark" *Architecture*. November 1925.

Lockwood, Charles. *Manhatten Moves Uptown*. Boston: Houghton Mifflin, 1976.

Lord & Taylor. *The New Store of Lord & Taylor*. New York, 1914.

Mahoney, Tom, and Leonard Sloane. *The Great Merchants*. 2d ed. New York: Harper & Row, 1966.

Marcus, Leonard S. *The American Store Window*. New York: Whitney Library of Design, 1978.

Matthews, Brander. *Vignettes of Manhattan: Outlines in Local Color*. New York: Scribner's, 1921.

Maurice, Arthur Bartlett. *Fifth Avenue*. New York: Dodd, Mead, 1918.

"Middle Fifth Avenue," *Real Estate Record and Guide*. April 20, 1901.

Moorehouse, Geoffrey. *The Imperial City: The Rise and Rise of New York*. London: Hodder & Stoughton, 1988.

Mumford, Lewis. "The Skyline," *The New Yorker*. November 20, 1937.

"The New Fifth Avenue," *Real Estate Record and Guide*. December 17, 1904.

New York City Landmarks Preservation Commission Designation Reports.

Palmer, Gretta. *A Shopping Guide to New York*. New York: Robert McBride & Co., 1930.

Price, C. Matlack. "A Renaissance in Commercial Architecture," *Architectural Record*. May 1912.

Reilly, Philip J. *Old Masters of Retailing*. New York: Fairchild Publications, Inc., 1966.

"Remodeling for Lord & Taylor," *Architectural Forum*. March 1938.

Rider, Fremont. *Rider's New York City*. New York: Henry Holt & Co., 1923.

Rinzler, Alan, ed. *The New York Spy*. New York: David White Co., 1967.

Roshco, Bernard. *The Rag Race*. New York: Funk & Wagnalls, 1963.

Schactman, Tom. *Skyscraper Dreams: The Great Real Estate Dynasties of New York*. Boston: Little, Brown & Co., 1991.

Scott, Mel. *American Planning Since 1890*. Berkeley, Calif.: University of California Press, 1971.

Shaver, Dorothy. *The Story of New York: An Island Fantasy*. New York: 1955.

Silver, Nathan. *Lost New York*. New York: Schocken Books, 1971.

Simon, Kate. *Fifth Avenue: A Very Social History*. New York: Harcourt Brace Jovanovich, 1978.

Stern, Robert A. M., Gregory Gilmartin, and John Montague Massengale. *New York: 1900*. New York: Rizzoli, 1983.

Stern, Robert A. M., Gregory Gilmartin, and Thomas Mellins. *New York: 1930*. New York: Rizzoli, 1987.

Tauranac, John, and Christopher Little. *Elegant New York*. New York: Abbeville Press, 1985.

Taylor, Alfred H. "Reconstructed Business House Fronts in New York," *Architectural Record*. July 1904.

Weiss, Marc A. "Skyscraper Zoning: New York's Pioneering Role," *Journal of the American Planning Association*. Spring 1992.

Willensky, Elliot, and Norval White. *AIA Guide to New York City*. 3d ed. San Diego: Harcourt Brace Jovanovich, 1988.

Wolfe, Gerard R. *New York: A Guide to the Metropolis: Walking Tours of Architecture and History*. New York: McGraw-Hill, 1988.

Worden, Helen. *Here Is New York*. New York: Doubleday, Doran & Co., 1939.

Worden, Helen. *The Real New York*. Indianapolis: Bobbs Merrill, 1932

Works Progress Administration. *W.P.A. Guide to New York City*. New York: Random House, 1939.

Zeisloft, E. Idell, ed. *The New Metropolis*. New York: Appleton, 1899.

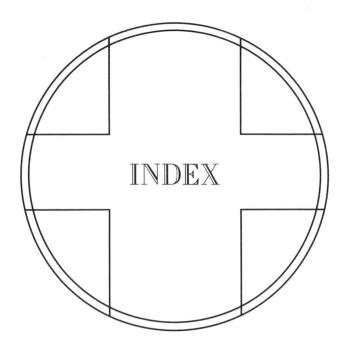

INDEX

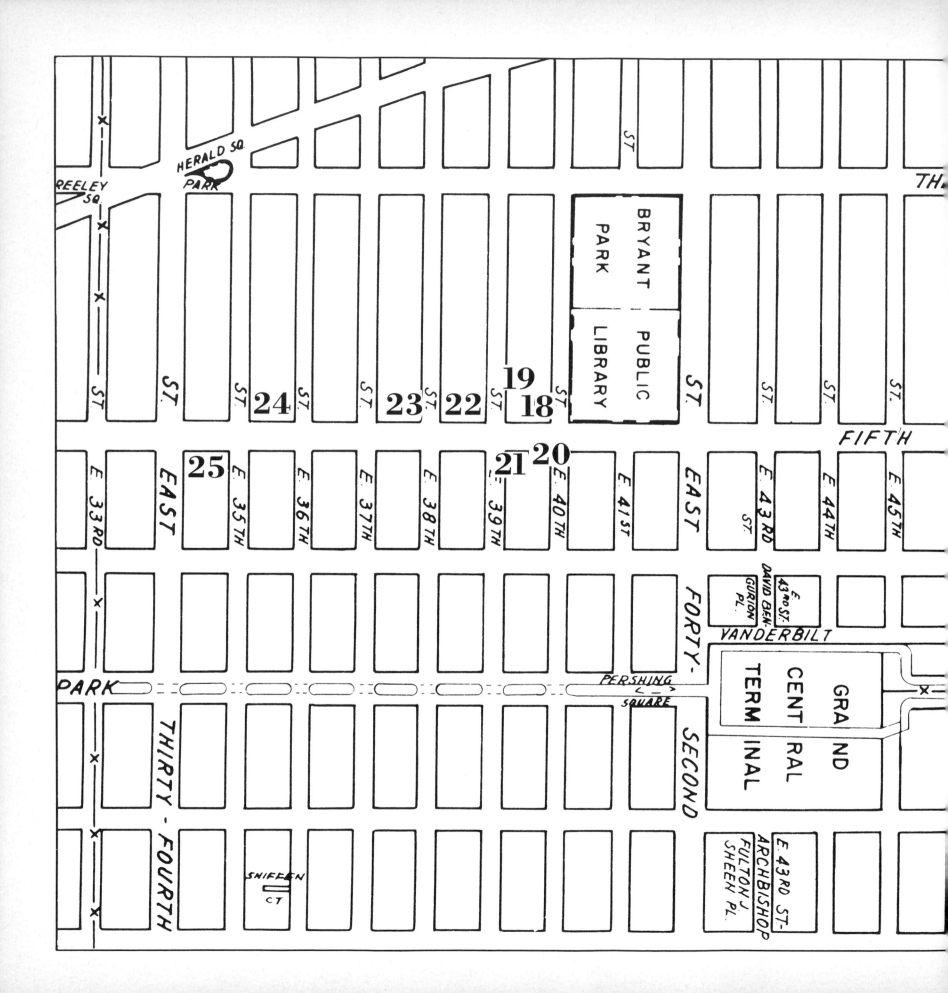

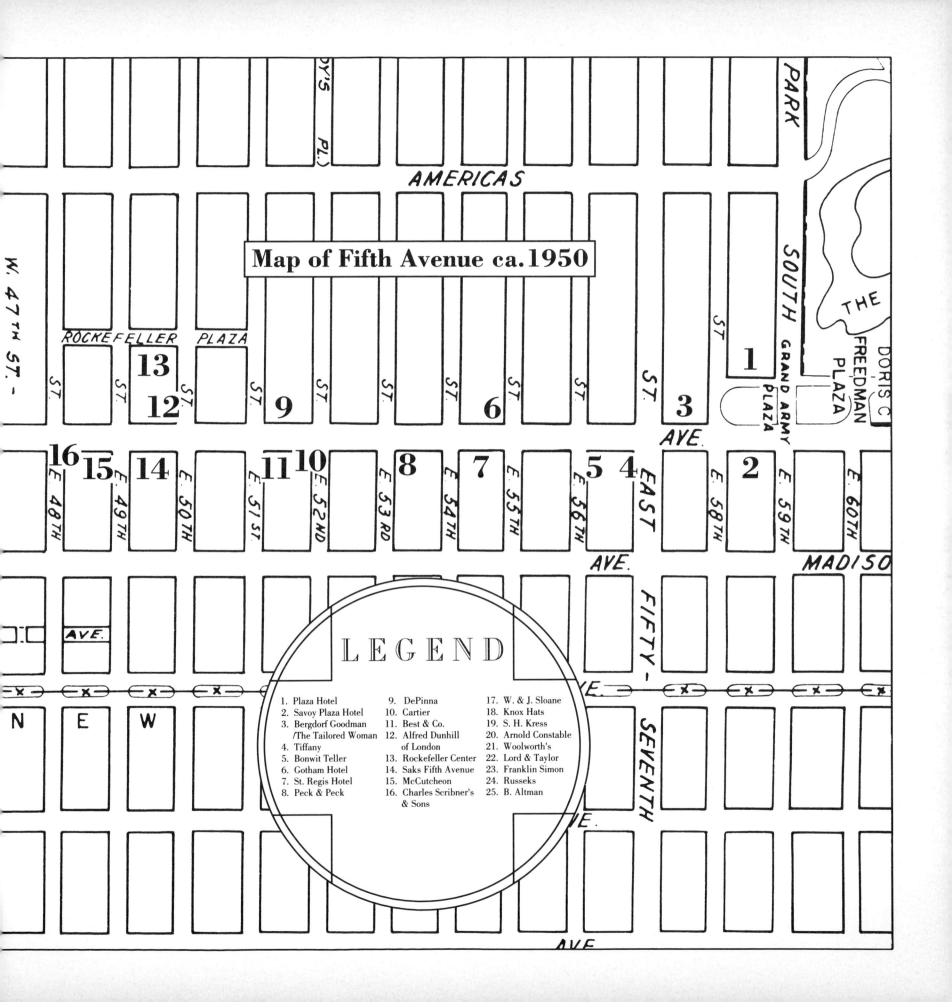

Map of Fifth Avenue ca. 1950

LEGEND

1. Plaza Hotel
2. Savoy Plaza Hotel
3. Bergdorf Goodman /The Tailored Woman
4. Tiffany
5. Bonwit Teller
6. Gotham Hotel
7. St. Regis Hotel
8. Peck & Peck
9. DePinna
10. Cartier
11. Best & Co.
12. Alfred Dunhill of London
13. Rockefeller Center
14. Saks Fifth Avenue
15. McCutcheon
16. Charles Scribner's & Sons
17. W. & J. Sloane
18. Knox Hats
19. S. H. Kress
20. Arnold Constable
21. Woolworth's
22. Lord & Taylor
23. Franklin Simon
24. Russeks
25. B. Altman